Michael Tomkinson's
TUNISIA

with eighty photographs by Jacques Perez

First published 1985 by
Michael Tomkinson Publishing,
POB. 215, Oxford OX2 0NR
Seventh edition 1995
Third reprinting with revised
illustrations 1999

© Michael Tomkinson 1985, 1999

Designed by Roger Davies
and Susan Kenning

Printed in Singapore by
Star Standard Industries
ISBN 0 905500 09 1

Contents

Introduction

Designed as a companion volume to my *Tunisia a Holiday Guide* and *Essential Tunisia*, this pictorial record of the country's attractions has in some respects become a requiem.

The photographs have been taken with the help of Jacques Perez in the course of the last twenty years. And Tunisia in those two decades has been physically transformed. The grass-roots growth of the 1970s continues – new settlements and suburbs, clinics, schools and low-cost homes – but with the 1980s came a spate of prestige projects: motorways and two new tram-cum-railways, nationwide industrial zones, city-centre skyscrapers and the Arab League headquarters, dams, canals and international pipe-lines, lavish tourist complexes, more international airports and splendid pleasure ports. It is no longer babies but building sites that characterize the new Tunisia.

The camera, we know, does not lie. Most of the views reproduced in this book remain unchanged and will, one hopes, survive the 1990s. Others I have retained, unashamedly, in the hope that the visitor, like the photographer, will be able to 'see selectively'; to appreciate an ancient site despite the shanties rising around it, and so detach, visually,

El-Jem, the amphitheatre

each feature of beauty or interest from its present-day, less decorative surroundings.

Irrespective of region, the people of Tunisia are so literally many-faced as to defy generalization. The country has since earliest times been a meeting-place of Middle Eastern and Mediterranean peoples and subject at certain periods to large-scale European penetration. The divers colours of skin, eyes and hair alone bear witness to the fact that the invading armies, whether Scipio's or Earl Alexander's, have left behind them not only destruction.

Most of the invasions – Phoenician, Roman, Vandal, Byzantine, Arab, Spanish, Turkish and finally French – were followed by periods of settlement. Their legacy to modern Tunisia is a concentration of historical sites more intensive than anywhere else in Africa. The abundance of Roman cities is such that the first to be excavated are now overgrown again, while the experts are very far from working on the last.

Place-names in Tunisia are of Arabic, Berber, Latin or Punic origin and, save for the few places mentioned in early European records, were formerly written in Arabic script alone. From 1881 to 1956 Tunisia was in theory 'protected', in fact ruled, by the French who, in drawing up the first maps and gazetteers, often committed the linguistic atrocity of adopting not the correct form of place-names but that used locally by the inhabitants, or even that which they, the French, could more easily pronounce. The result is like a map of London with the place-names transcribed in Cockney. As it would only confuse the traveller to give other spellings I have, reluctantly, left these Gallic 'Ammersmiffs.

Tunisia is no longer a novelty for European travellers. Launched in the mid-1960s as a popular holiday destination, it soon deserved its permanent place in most travel brochures. Some 300 custom-built hotels now house, feed, transport and entertain an annual total of around three million visitors.

Crossing the Chott el-Jerid

Common Tunisian and/or Arabic Terms

Bab 'Door' in Arabic, used for the monumental and easily defensible town-gates set in the walls of each medina; also, sometimes, for the districts surrounding c.f. Tunis' Bab Souika and Bab Carthagène.

Ben (pl. Beni) The North African version of the Arabic *ibn* (son of) e.g. Mohammed ibn Abdallah; in places used without the first name for a location founded by or associated with the son: Ben Arous, Ben Metir.

Bou The Arabic *abu* (father of) corrupted and misspelt by the Maghreb peoples and the French respectively; used, like *ben*, in place-names: Sidi Bou Said. *Bou/abu* may denote not only paternity but possession: Jebel Bou Kornine, the Mountain with two Peaks.

Chott A salt-flat or large sebkha (below). The Tunisian chotts, stretching from the Gulf of Gabes 200 miles west into Algeria, and in places lower than sea-level, form a distinctive geological feature on the northern fringe of the Sahara.

Dar/Diar 'House/houses' in Arabic.

Fondouk The Arabic for 'hotel', spelt correctly *funduq*. The funduqs of Tunisia however are the quarters allotted by the Hafsite rulers, inside or outside the medina, to early European merchants and envoys.

Ghorfa 'Room' in Arabic, but in Tunisia the long, vaulted, multi-storey chambers built of rock and mud, and usually on an eminence, as depots for the produce of the Beduin in the south-east.

Hammam (pl. Hammamet) 'Bath' in Arabic, the white-domed 'Turkish bath', a sanitary and social institution which villagers, carrying their towels and *tfal* (mud shampoo) in a suitcase, visit with exemplary frequency. The chambers of increasing heat, with massage-rooms and final restrooms, are similar in function, if inferior in style, to those of the Roman thermae.

Kasba Unrelated, *pace* Hollywood, to shaikh ('old man' in Arabic) or harem (which merely means 'women'); in fact the bastioned and battlemented stronghold, usually at the highest point of the medina, where the garrison was quartered and the townspeople sought refuge from invaders.

Koubba The Arabic 'cupola', properly spelt *qubba*; a generic term for any domed marabout or tourbet.

Spring flowers in Hammamet

Ksar (pl. Ksour) 'Castle' or 'palace' in Arabic, but in south-east Tunisia a hill-top settlement consisting of ghorfas built in a defensive square.

Marabout The word *murabit* (see Ribat) modified in North Africa, and in the course of time, to mean 'saint' or 'holy man'. Revered for wisdom, piety or merely mental oddity, each local marabout is finally interred in a square domed shrine also called a marabout.

Medina Arabic for 'town' or 'civilized place' and used nowadays in North Africa for the originally high-walled, narrow-alleyed burgh around which first the Turkish, then the French-protectorate conurbation grew.

Menzel Strictly *manzil*, meaning in Arabic a 'house', 'home' or 'resting place', and used in Tunisia for both permanent settlement sites – Menzel Bourguiba, Menzel Temime – and the low, gabled workshops of Jerba.

Oued The French rendering of the Arabic *wadi*, translatable only as 'valley'; any linear depression, usually formed by but rarely bearing water, and varying in size from a ditch to a ravine.

Ouled The Arabic *awlaad* (sons of) as transcribed by the French; used, like *ben* and *bou*, in 'patronymic' place-names.

Ribat From the Arabic *rabata* (to bind); a monastery-fortress in which the early *murabitin* (those 'bound' to Islam) lived, prayed and prepared themselves for martyrdom fighting the Christian 'infidels'.

Sebkha A barren salt-depression, frequent in North Africa and Arabia; geologically, a deposit of gypsum and anhydrite formed by the salt of underground seepages rising and mixing with the surface sand and mud.

Sidi The North African corruption of *Sayyidi*, literally 'My lord' but actually just 'Sir' in Arabic. Often corrupted even further to *Si*, it corresponds, in addressing a man by name, to Mr e.g. Si Mohammed.

Souk The Arabic *suq*, a market or market-place.

Tourbet In Arabic 'earth', 'dust' or 'holy ground' and in Tunisia, equally correctly, a 'burial place'; usually the mausoleum of a civic or religious dignitary, larger and more lavishly domed than a marabout.

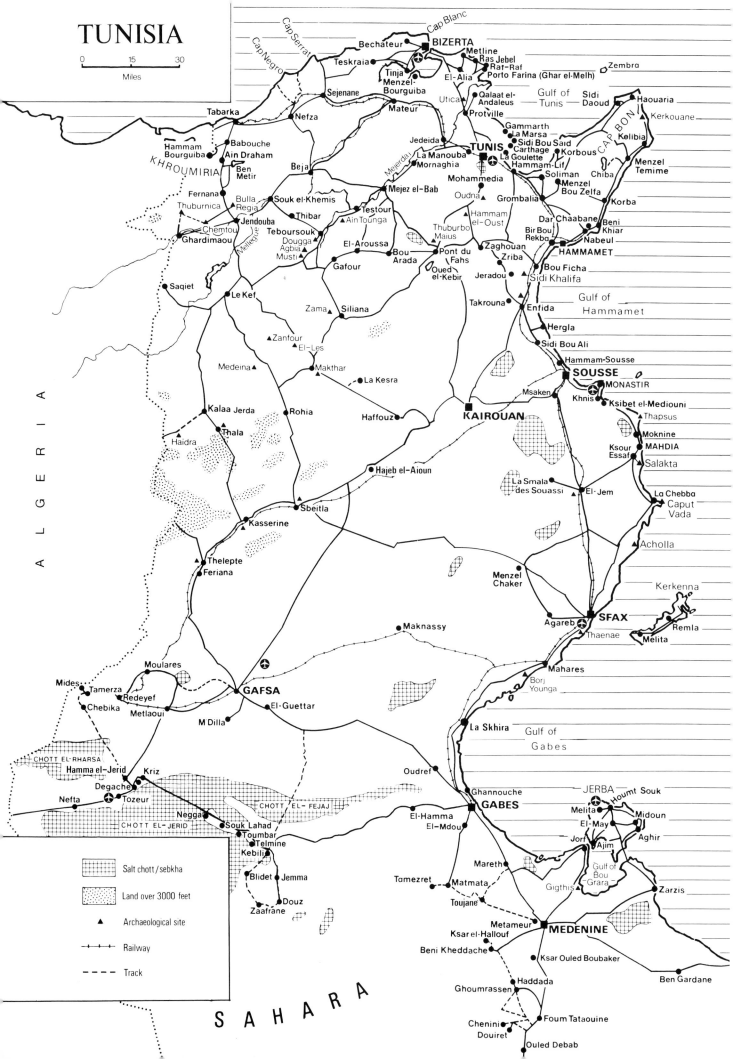

Geography. Tunisia is the northernmost country of Africa and comparable in size to the UK without Scotland: 63,378 square miles. Facing east with a mostly low Mediterranean coast scalloped by the three large Gulfs of Tunis, Hammamet and Gabes, it backs in the west on to Algeria and the Atlas Mountains. With the Algerian frontier very roughly parallel to the eastern seaboard, the average east-west width is 150 miles. The short north coast rises to the Cap Blanc promontory by Bizerta, and the Saharan frontier-post of Borj el-Hattaba lies 500 miles due south.

Along the north coast runs the panhandle of a rugged mountain chain, from the Ain Draham forests of cork-oak and pine to the twin lakes of Bizerta and Ichkeul. Southwards, the meandering and very fertile Mejerda Valley divides this region from the undulating farmlands of the central *Tell* ('Plateau'). To the east the Tell peters out, firstly into low wheat country that stretches from Bizerta to the capital, Tunis; then, beyond the 'corridor' that leads down to Hammamet (and was once a sea-channel between Africa and Europe), into Cap Bon (geologically a part of Sicily, from which it is only 87 miles distant), and finally into the *Sahel* ('Shore') of Sousse. To the south and west the Tell rises into the *Dorsale* range, Tunisia's 'Backbone'.

From the well-watered Mediterranean north, Tunisia then sinks, unevenly, towards the Sahara. In the centre is the steppe region, rich only in Roman remains, interrupted in the west by Jebel Chambi (5066 feet and the country's highest peak) and merging in the east with the unbroken miles of olive-groves that are the Sahel of Sfax. A line of arid hills across from Metlaoui to Maknassy makes one last stand before the desert. There is a scattering of islands round the 810-mile coast, some little known and uninhabited, others as popular as Jerba.

Tunisia's Sahara starts with the chotts. These salt-flats are frequently quagmires in winter, but spectacular curiosities in summer. Then the

Saharan palms at sunset

The north coast near Tabarka

salt of the viscous sand-mud mix dries to form a firm crust that shimmers crystalline white for miles, and often resolves into a mirage. On terra firma beside the chotts stand the oases: exotic, on-shore islands of palms, pools, camels and general picturesqueness that not even travel brochures need exaggerate.

There is one more fascinating diversion: the dramatic rise of the Matmatas and the Ksour – bald, russet, mostly table-top summits that until recently sheltered Berber cave-dwellers, pit-dwellers and cliff-dwellers. Then the dunes take over. With little more of interest save the name – Great Eastern Erg – Tunisia runs out in the sands of the Sahara.

Climate.

The varied topography inevitably affects both temperature and rainfall. Broadly speaking, the north is Mediterranean-warm, the south Saharan-hot, but coastal resorts both north and south are tempered by perennial sea-breezes that make the summer sun enjoyable for the tenderest skins and the winter weather generally fine for every outdoor activity save swimming.

Summer temperatures can rise in places to over 40°C, although the August average for the last 50 years is 30° in Sousse, 29° in Tabarka, 30° in Hammamet, 30° on Jerba and 32° in Tozeur, the most Saharan of Tunisian towns. Tunisia's climate has of late, however, been proving almost British in its unpredictability. In 1969, and 1986 again, September was calamitous with floods; that month in 1993 had a heat wave. February 1973 was immemorially miserable, February 1990 was sunny and mild, and in 1978 and 1995 it saw the end of a long hot drought. By March spring is usually sprung: for one freakish week in 1981 holiday-makers in Hammamet built snowmen on the beach.

Everywhere May and June seem the most enjoyable months: flowers bloom the year round but then the colours and abundance are delightful. July and August are best for serious sun-tanning, although half-days of rain come as a regular surprise. In autumn the air and the sea are as limpid and warm as in spring; only the greenery has dulled in the summer sun. November rains can vary from momentary showers to cloud-bursts. And in winter, which can start as early as October or as late as December and give way to Hot and Dry any time between February and April, one can shiver in bright sunshine or be warm in a thunderstorm.

Agriculture.

Though tourism and petroleum now earn for Tunisia far more than does agriculture, crops, if not livestock, have always been a mainstay of the economy. Since Neolithic man first took to cultivation here, growing wheat, beans, chick-peas, turnips, melons and even garlic, farming has sustained the population, attracted covetous neighbours from the Phoenicians to the French, and often transformed the landscape.

On the hills and plains of the centre and north, fields of wheat dictate the colour of the terrain: spring-green, rolling gold, burned autumn stubble and winter ploughed brown. Hard wheat, the Berbers' ancient *irden*, made of Egypt and Tunisia the 'granary of Rome'. Hard wheat together with Mexican varieties, maize, sorghum, oats, rye and barley, occupies an area of 4,148,980 acres and in 1994 yielded 1,914,000 tonnes.

The Phoenicians terraced, in Levantine fashion, the eroded slopes of eastern Tunisia and there planted vines. Promoted by the Romans for their excellent wines, maintained by the Muslims only for their grapes, the vineyards flourished, predictably, under the French (who protected their own and Italian *colons* by legislation against Tunisian growers).

On Jerba wild olives were in prehistoric times already pressed for oil. The Phoenicians introduced the cultivated *olea*, and the monolithic presses to be seen on every site show how the Romans developed it on an almost industrial scale. (They used the oil only for heating and lighting, though, considering it too coarse for consumption.) The legacy today is the 50 million trees that annually yield 75,000 tonnes of oil, place Tunisia sixth amongst world exporters of olive-oil, and make a drive across the Sahel so astonishingly boring.

Whether here in their well-aligned but never ending rows or in gnarled, unwatered groves across the country, the olive-trees are harvested laboriously by hand: fitting a small sheep's horn to each finger, the pickers scale the trees to scrape the boughs and drop the fruit into a *futa* spread below.

In the Mountains of the Ksour

Where, on the Cap Bon coast, the cloches and plastic hot-houses stop, the citrus groves begin: some grapefruit, better lemons (even sweet, as the *beldi*) and, above all, oranges. From October to May, in a dozen successive varieties, 207,000 tonnes of Valencia and Maltaise oranges, clementines and mandarines are collected, graded and packed for export in Menzel Bou Zelfa and Soliman, Beni Khalled and Hammamet. Strawberries ripen in April and May, followed by apricots and melons, peaches and figs, then grapes and pomegranates . . .

Wheatfields of central Tunisia (left), the 'granary of Rome'

Esparto grass or alfa (not the same as American alfalfa) grows scrubbily on the stony central steppe. Over 1,070,000 acres in fact, and the women that pick it, bent double all day, deliver some 36,000 tonnes each year. A British concern obtained the first concession to work Tunisia's alfa in the late 19th century. The bales seen nowadays stacked by southern roadsides go either to Sfax for export or to the factory at Kasserine for processing into cellulose or crude cardboard and paper.

Alfa worked on Kerkenna makes Sfax's fishing-port picturesque, while in recent years homes around Hergla's mosque have turned into booths selling the dry-green matting, bags and lidded baskets.

The date-palm is a native of Saharan Africa and Asia from India to the Canaries. Grown only ornamentally in northern Tunisia, it dominates the oases of the south and meets most of the oasis-dwellers' needs. The cash-crop of dates in the 1993-94 season totalled 86 million kilos, the choice *Deglat Nur* ('Fingers of Light') being the best of a dozen varieties.

In 1957 phylloxera eradicated most of the original cultures, and the country's 27,200 acres of vineyards have since been replanted with Californian strains. Around Grombalia in particular one can see the winter vines cut back like tufted candlewick and, in August and September, the workers loading the tractor-trailers high with grapes for the private and co-operative presseries.

Mosaics in the Bardo Museum are beautiful Roman records of the vegetables and fruit served at Tunisian tables 2000 years ago: from broad beans to the curious gombo/okra, *alias* 'lady's finger'; from figs and grapes to pomegranates, which the Romans nicknamed 'Punic apples' (and Tunisians call *ruman*). There followed bananas, small and sweet from the oases, and – via the Spanish from the Americas – tomatoes, potatoes and especially pimentoes/red peppers. No Tunisian meal, it seems, is complete without the last. Alongside the full range of market-garden produce, they are grown mostly in the Mejerda Valley and Cap Bon.

Amid and around the cash-crops grow the functional, 'back-up' species: cypress, eucalyptus, cactus and agave. The first two came in with the French. Fast-growing, they serve as wind-breaks, their roots holding water – and the soil against erosion. Tunisia's eucalyptus, one of 50 originally Australian species, also shade the road admirably, if dangerously, in every part of the country. Saplings are planted in the south to keep back sand-dunes from the farm-plots, and branches hung on house-walls in Sfax are supposedly an insect deterrent. So-called 'mimosas' (really acacias) also fix the soil, and become in spring a resplendence of yellow, particularly around Carthage but equally as far south as Gabes.

The *aloès* or agave is easily recognized, each plant throwing up one monstrous but characteristic 'stick' before it dies. Here it is neither decorticated for sisal nor pressed into tequila, but used exclusively in the *tabia* (hedge) which keeps livestock off the crops. The ubiquitous cactus is a more effective barrier. Brought over from the Americas by the Spanish in the 16th century, the 'Barbary fig' or 'prickly pear' has ferocious prickles offset by gorgeous summer flowers. Its fig/pear is a bready, juiceless fruit which notwithstanding sustains the southern Beduin in time of drought. Demarcating, almost defending every smallholding, the tabias are a symbol of the peasant's pride of ownership.

Government. Tunisia is a republic, independent and headed by President Zine el-Abidine Ben Ali. A former general, ambassador and prime minister, he succeeded Tunisia's first president, Habib Bourguiba, in a peaceful and constitutional deposition on 7 November 1987. It is Ben Ali's portrait that one sees hanging in hotels, shops and homes. Bourguiba, born in 1903, had founded the country's principal political party, the Destour, in 1934; had led it through two anti-French decades of demonstrations, subversion, wholesale imprisonment and final independence of France in March 1956, and had dictated almost every step since in the development of this, the most sophisticated, tolerant and relaxed state in North Africa.

The republic is divided into 23 *gouvernorats*, in which a *gouverneur* or *wali* is the president's right-hand man. The next tone down in the administrative scale is the *délégation* or *mu'tamadia*; a governorate (*wilaya* in Arabic) consists of from three to fourteen; in each of the country's 270-odd delegations, a *délégué* or *mu'tamad* represents the governor. Places such as Sousse, Monastir and Nabeul are *sièges* ('county towns') of governorates of the same name in the immediate hinterland; lesser towns like Hammamet and Tabarka, or rural areas like Jerba, are delegations. The local *baladia* or *municipalité* does the work of a British town council, the *rais el-baladia* (mayor) being responsible for the borough services and questions of personal status.

The *Habib*, pride of the Tunisian fleet, arriving at La Goulette

Nabeul, the Friday Market

Population. How young a country Tunisia is soon becomes very obvious, if only from the crowds of pink- or blue-smocked children off to school at apparently any hour of day. For the bulk of the country, education began with independence. When the French left in 1956, only one in four children eligible for school was actually attending; within ten years the figure had trebled, and in September 1994 a new school-year started for 1,472,844 primary and 662,222 secondary schoolchildren.

At the last national census in 1994, Tunisia had a population of 8,785,304 and a serious problem with it. With 48% aged less than twenty, 95% of school-age children receiving education (at a cost of one third of the country's budget) and the percentage of adult unemployment significantly undisclosed, family planning remains as crucial an economic issue here as inflation and interest rates at home.

A successful exception in the Third World, however, Tunisia can congratulate itself on having defused the demographic time-bomb. Population growth has peaked and, at 2·3% per annum, is now in a controlled decline. Thanks to a concerted (and often ingenious) campaign, the country's family-planning authorities have largely overcome traditional family patterns, entrenched religious attitudes and natural inclinations in a warm and sunny land. The baby boom of the 1960s has worked through to maturity and home-ownership, and thus caused the current building boom.

Formerly large families were a way of life (as still they are in certain rural areas). Parents often thought, too, in terms of allowing for losses when high infant mortality resulted from malaria, tuberculosis and typhoid. Until this socializing state can afford old age pensions for all, some parents cannot be expected to stop working energetically for an early retirement.

Although they may be noisy, impertinent and everywhere, Tunisian children are rarely short of adorable. In the towns, especially, the mixture of races results in surprisingly widespread good looks, bright minds and attractive personalities. British and American visitors to this 'developing' country are repeatedly taken aback by children who speak Arabic as their mother tongue, are usually bilingual in French by their mid-teens and often go on to fluency in English, German, Italian, Spanish or apparently any language that bazaar business requires.

In Khroumiria, purple mellia

Origins. Tunisia's aborigines were the Berbers, about whom a good deal has been written but little is known. Herodotus describes some of their tribes: the Atlantes who 'eat no living creature and never dream'; the Atarantes, 'the only people in the world to do without names', and the Gindanes whose 'womenfolk wear leather bands round their ankles, one for each of their lovers'. But this is just early journalism. What few reliable findings there are suggest a typically colourful beginning: that about 10,000 BC a dark-haired, brown-skinned people settled in and around Tunisia, subsequently interbreeding with both Negroes from the Sahara and mysterious, blue-eyed, blond-haired immigrants from the north. The variegated offspring called themselves *Imazighen* (Noble Ones) but the Romans called them *Barbari* (Uncouth) and this name has, perhaps unjustly, stuck.

Tourists, and even Tunisians, sometimes confuse the terms Beduin and Berber. The latter, as we have seen, is an ethnographic expression. *Beduin* is the plural – c.f. *cherub/cherubim* – of the Arabic *bedui* ('belonging to the desert'). Because desert-dwellers are pastoralists, moving with the grazing for their herds, 'Beduin' has come to be synonymous with 'nomad'. And because many Berber groups were and still are nomads, the two terms are loosely used as one.

The Romans recognized the Berber sub-divisions that modern ethnologists accept: the Libyci of Egypt, Libya and southern Tunisia, the Numidae of western Tunisia and Algeria, and the Mauri of Morocco and Mauretania. Though usually fragmented into semi-nomadic groups, the Berbers were rallied by energetic kings such as Massinissa, Syphax, Jugurtha and Juba into a rich, wheat-exporting nation whose well-trained armies played, for example, an underrated part in the Punic Wars.

When not united in opposition, the Berber tribes took refuge from foreign aggressors on islands like Jerba, in the remoter mountain fastnesses of the Matmatas and the Ksour or behind the lines in isolated, easily defended eagle's nests such as Jeradou, Zriba and Takrouna. How much they intermarried with the invaders and settlers is a matter of academic dispute: 'The Arabs at least must have intermarried', writes Sir Geoffrey Furlonge, 'because their armies arrived and settled without wives'.

Home from market, a southern oasis

Frequent male accoutrements:
red chechia and posy of jasmin

Burnus and white kafia:
everyday wear in the south

On the central steppe, with Beduin
silver bracelet, necklace and fibulas

Douz, armed horseman at
the Festival du Sahara

Nabeul, the Habib Bourguiba Mosque

Religion. Most Tunisians are Muslim. But no more or less so than the British are Christian. Except during Ramadhan (a moveable, month-long fast when Muslims should refrain from all indulgence by day) and in mosques (where a decree in 1972 put the prayer-room out of bounds to non-Muslims) Islam does not affect holidays. It adds to them in fact a touch of exoticism, the muezzin intoning the call to prayer five times each day, and a measure of beauty, for the mosques still being built in many a town and village are as ornate and well proportioned as the traditional edifices everywhere. Two *madhab*s (Islamic schools of thought) rule here: square minarets denote mosques of the Malikite sect, octagonal those of the Hanifite. Both being orthodox Sunnites, the adherents of one pray in mosques of the other; only the Kharijites of Jerba and the Sufis are viewed slightly askance.

One of ex-President Bourguiba's several secular reforms in 1957 align-ed Tunisia with Europe by establishing Sunday, rather than the Muslim Friday, as the weekly day of rest. But in parts of the interior the old ways still prevail; even city supermarkets may not sell liquor on Fridays, and shopkeepers in the seaside resorts, like the self-employed everywhere, work every day of the week.

Islamic fatalism – all is *maktub*, Written – may, with the Tunisians' inherent friendliness, explain their edifying attitude to life. The middle class of the cities here now lives, drives and dresses in modern and prosperous style. Thousands, however, do not share that affluence. The minimum agricultural wage is £2·50 per day and many, simply for the sake of work, accept less. Their morale could be a lesson for the West, where standards tend to be measured in material things. If prosperity were measured in contentment, hospitality and family solidarity regardless of what was earned, possessed or looked forward to, Tunisia might be giving aid to Europe.

Again an odd-man-out in the Arab world, Tunisia has Jewish communities co-existing peacefully. They are still considerable in and around the capital. Jerba has a synagogue, the Ghriba, more famous than the functional concrete piles in Tunis and Sfax, but less Jews than the travel books say. Long-established colonies are to be found in the interior too: the 'Andalusian' village of Testour has a Hebrew cemetery with some up-to-date insertions, and only in 1983 the last Jew left Le Kef, leaving the ceremonial silverware to the regional museum.

Sfax, the Great Mosque

Monastir, courtyard of the
Habib Bourguiba Mosque

19

Architecture. The domes and minarets of the mosques are as much a central feature of each Tunisian town or village as church spires once were in Britain. Usually elegant, tasteful and exotic, they epitomize a style of architecture everywhere impressive: white spires and arches, white domes, walls and cupolas, with the sky-blue of doors and mashrabias. The palaces of the beys, the former monarchs, may be not painted blue but tiled blue with façades of fine ceramic: although red and white are Tunisia's national colours, it is blue and white that characterize the country.

White to combat the heat, blue as an insect repellent, domes to help the cool air circulate inside . . . Tunisian designers are sensibly aesthetic. Hotels were built and furnished until recently with the Tunisian look: low, clean lines, apparent simplicity and strong pastel shades that white walls accept and soften. This modestly delightful style blends well with the gardens of Hammamet, the olive-groves of Sousse and Jerba's beaches.

Massive aid and investment from the Arab oil states, plus the overall improvement in the economy, have however enabled building to become something of a national sport. And official laissez-faire has meant that uniformity of style has been abandoned (except at the lower end of the scale where, in every suburb and rural centre, the rock-and-rough-plastered shops and homes seem never-finished and uniformly ugly).

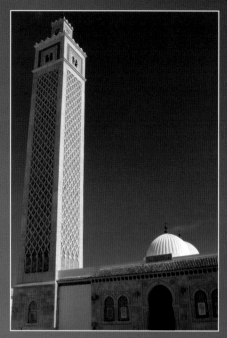

Marabout's tomb near Douz (left)
Minaret of the Habib Bourguiba Mosque,
Nabeul (upper left)
Interior of the 'Barber's Mosque',
Kairouan (right)
Date depôt, Degache (upper right)
Patio of the Dar el-Oula, Tunis Medina
(centre)

Dress. Women's dress does not, as many visitors believe, depend on their marital state, although especially elaborate wear does exist for weddings. The Museums of Popular Arts and Traditions in Tunis, Le Bardo, Sfax, Moknine, Houmt Souk, Gabes, Tozeur and Le Kef have excellent collections of the dozens of regional types. (There are ceremonial suits, too, for better-class boys on their circumcision day. The event is still indispensable for every young Muslim but use of the costume grows less.)

The *sifsari* is the white cloak-cum-wrap-cum-shawl one sees women wearing everywhere. The sifsari's woollen counterpart is the *ha'ik*, usually white or grey but an attractive black with red fringes in the villages beyond Monastir. These are outdoor garments and worn as a rule over Western-style clothes.

In many country areas, and especially those with Berber blood, women's dress is entirely indigenous. It starts with a long slip called *suria* or *meriul*. The *mellia* (a sari-type drape sometimes six yards long) is wound round the waist and held over the bust by large silver fibulas (*khlal*) that pin the front of the mellia below each shoulder like dungaree braces. A thickly wound belt called *hizam*, often no more than a skein of dyed wool, supports new mothers' midriffs. Many village women go more simply clad in a *futa* (skirt) and *blusa*, and poorer Beduin women will often combine the mellia and the futa in a single strip of cloth, which rather resembles the *chlamyde* worn by ancient Greeks. The mellia, like the caftan and the popular, sleeveless, shift-shaped *jebba* or *thaub*, is now inspiring Western designers.

Reds predominate, especially in the Sahel. Inland and in the oases, both Beduin and townswomen prefer more subdued purple and blue, but in the Khroumiria Mountains vivid purple is common. The variations in dress, from the witches' hats of straw they wear on Jerba to the gold bangles, anklets, pendants and teeth that are the Beduin housewife's life-savings, are legion.

Men's dress is usually less colourful. In everyday life educated Tunisians wear Western attire (to which the elder gentry add a red fez, the *tarbush*). Most characteristic amongst the less educated are the *chechia*s: bright red, round and peakless felt hats, part-pillbox part-beret, once imported from Czechoslovakia, now mostly made in the Tunis Medina.

In the north labourers by and large wear blue two-piece worksuits. For farm-workers elsewhere the popular *jellaba* is the Egyptian *galabia*: a plain, practical, long-sleeved, ankle-length shirt. The *burnus* is a full- or half-length topcoat that is made from wool or camel-hair, with or without hood and usually in the animal's natural colours. Similar but commoner now is the *kashabia*, woollen, hooded and frequently striped. Its Jerban counterpart is the *kabaya* which, with its open front and crudely pointed hood, looks like nothing so much as a split sack. The town's answer to all this is the delightful *gondura*, which has the dignity of a graduate's gown and the comfort of a nightshirt – a silken, airy garment that well-to-do Tunisians wear in summer. Only certain ageing labourers, and the merchants of Jerba and the Sahel, still wear the *sirwal*: the unspeakably baggy outer breeches which, like the gondura, leave the lower half of the calf exposed above the sock or the *babouche*, the heelless slipper.

Instead of the chechia many villagers wear the *mudhala* ('sunshade'), a tall, broad-rimmed straw hat (that on Roman slaves was called *petasus*). The *kafia*, the Lawrence-of-Arabia headcloth, can be seen in the south, but usually without the band around. When this, the *kishta*, is worn white, green or gold round a red fez it denotes religious rank.

Everyday wear for work, near Kasserine

The Sahel, with a hizam round the usually red dress, by a *tabia* (hedge) of prickly pear

Washing wool in the sea near
Houmt Souk
Berber beauties at a village wedding
(right & below)

In Kairouan, clad in a black ha'ik

Black Tunisians, frequently seen
in the south

24

Women. At the time of independence Tunisia was, in brochure-talk, still The Land of the Veil. From puberty until old age women kept their faces as strictly covered as everything else. They were rarely educated, had their husbands chosen for them, often shared him with two or three other wives, had no right of divorce and were not even accepted as court-case witnesses unless a man endorsed their evidence. There are stories from the 1950s of girls committing suicide rather than accept their parents' choice of husband, or being stabbed by fathers or brothers for the slightest pre-marital dalliance.

When people look back on Habib Bourguiba's work today, they usually agree that two revolutionary social reforms stand out as invaluable and irrevocable. One is universal education; the other, women's emancipation. Within five months of independence a statute had enforced equality of the sexes. By 1960 polygamy had been abolished, although older husbands – presumably no longer a threat in the over-population problem – were allowed to keep their four wives. Girls' schools were multiplying, and with them the first mixed classes. Now, as Tunisians are only too proud to tell you, women are active everywhere.

Wedding, formal in the north

Drummer and dancing-men at a desert wedding

Marriage – and Relations. Until very recently girls rarely had much of a say in their marriage: except in certain either enlightened or disreputable families they could seldom circulate freely and select. This naturally restricted things for the Tunisian suitor too. Parents would accept it was time a son should marry (in late teens or early twenties); mothers and sisters would visit friends, neighbours and relatives with eligible daughters, and report. The family would discuss and, collectively, decide. The fathers then did the rest: a meeting to fix the bride-price, some discreet inquiries by the bride's father as to the young man's character and the young man's family to arrange and pay for the wedding.

Bourguiba's reforms, like the First World War in Europe, led to women going out to work alongside men, and to tabus being broken. In some villages cousins, in the old Islamic pattern, may still be automatically coupled, but everywhere else young Tunisians are free to meet, choose and woo. Their wedding remains none the less a week-long event, with the bride, first shaved ceremonially, loaded in her once-a-lifetime finery, the pipes and drums cacophonous, the kohl-eyed and henna-daubed women ululating and the gifts coming (sometimes) by camel-borne *johfa*.

Tunisia's past

Punic. Tunisia enters history, according to the cliché, with the Phoenicians. This Semitic people we know from the Bible – the natives of Sidon and Tyre – and from the history of Cornish tin trading. Like the British, the Phoenicians developed a commercial empire and likewise needed regular naval bases.

Their first strategic settlements along the Tunisian coast were at Outih (Utica), Hadrumetum (Sousse), Hippo Diarrhytus (Bizerta) and Thines (Tunis). These were at first purely trading stations, but the military significance of ports that controlled the narrow straits between the two halves of the Mediterranean, then the centre of the world, was soon to be recognized.

When the Assyrians invaded their homeland many Phoenicians fled westwards, and the history of this refugee movement has crystallized round the legendary Queen Dido. 'Elissa' was the sister of King Pygmalion of Tyre, who coveted her husband Acherbas' fortune. When Pygmalion had Acherbas killed, Elissa fled with the fortune, and with those Tyrians opposed to the king, first to Cyprus where, in order to perpetuate their number, they picked up 80 virgins destined for sacred prostitution, then on to Tunisia. Hereafter history calls Elissa 'Dido' (the Wanderer).

Rather than join an already established community, the immigrants founded Kart Hadasht (New Capital) in 814 BC. The local ruler Iarbus, the story goes, agreed to their occupying 'as much land as could be covered by the hide of a bull': whereupon Dido's men killed the largest bull, cut its hide into the thinnest shreds and stretched them all the way round what became the Hill of Byrsa (*byrsa*, in Greek, meaning hide). Iarbus then set his sights on Dido. She declined, risked the survival of her people by rebuffing this powerful local prince and solved the dilemma by mounting the epic funeral pile. It was Virgil, 700 years later, who paired her with Aeneas, overlooking the chronological fact that to have called at Carthage the Trojan hero must have lived to be over 400 years old.

There were centuries of rivalry with the Greeks, also seafaring and pressing westward, but Carthage flourished. Its explorers Himilco and Hanno sailed as far as the Irish Sea and south (so they claimed) to the Gulf of Guinea. Trade followed. Monuments, tombs and *tophets* indicate that at home Carthaginian (Punic) control spread from present-day Tabarka to Sfax, and inland to Dougga and Makthar. The Carthaginians built cities which the Romans were to inherit, and marked the countryside with the Levantine system of terracing, which today explains why the slopes of the Atlas look in places like those of the Lebanon and Palestine. Apart from the 28 volumes of Mago's *Treatise on Agronomy* and Hanno's deliberately misleading account of his *Periplus*, what little literature we have on the Carthaginians is Latin: coming from a people that fought long and hard to destroy them, its reliability is a matter for conjecture.

Most of the archaeological evidence we have is of the Punic dead: the Romans obliteratd almost every trace of Carthage, but the dead survived as a clue to the Punic way of life. Their *tophets* or crematoriums, in Salammbo and Sousse, contain the ashes of hundreds of murdered children. Reliefs on certain steles (tombstones) indicate that the first-born boys and girls were not burned alive but first strangled in public, in *moloch*-sacrifice to the gods Melkart, Eshmun, Baal Hammon and Tanit, in times of national or personal misfortune.

The Carthaginians sacrificed children; they crucified defeated generals (and, incidentally, captive lions), presumably *pour encourager les autres*,

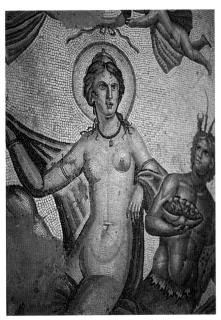

Roman mosaic of the goddess Amphitrite, Bulla Regia

Rome in Africa: Pheradi Maius
near Hammamet

and Roman writers describe them as 'cruel, cowardly, lecherous and over-ambitious'. Given which, it is sobering to think that the one battle of Zama alone stopped Carthage from overrunning the West and, instead of Rome, dictating the subsequent course of European civilization.

Sicily was a pawn repeatedly fought for by first Carthage and Greece, then Carthage and Rome. The pawn had even tried to decide its own fate when, in August of 310 BC, Agathocles invaded 'Africa' and defeated Carthage's mercenary army somewhere near the present Tunis International Airport. Within three years this 'Tyrant of Syracuse' had come near to taking Carthage. But the inhabitants took countermeasures, such as sacrificing 500 babies, and the gods restored their fortunes. Where Agathocles failed, the Romans were to succeed.

Stylized depiction of the Punic
goddess Tanit, Kerkouane

Popular history, like the popular press, prefers sensational disasters to uneventful prosperity, and the 'spectacular' Punic Wars are the best-known part of Carthage's past. The First Punic War (264-241BC) consisted mainly of naval engagements around Sicily: by copying a captured Carthaginian quinquereme and enlisting the seamen of Syracuse, the Romans for the first time took to the waves and beat the veteran Punic fleet at Milazzo. Despite Regulus' luckless invasion of Cap Bon, Rome triumphed again in 241 BC, forcing the Phoenicians out of Sicily.

Dependent on generals whom it usually mistrusted and relying on booty to pay its mercenary army, Carthage's oligarchy faced a multiple dilemma in defeat. Unwisely, the Magonite leaders repatriated 20,000 unpaid soldiers from Sicily to Le Kef. Talks not having settled the problem of their pay, the Revolt of the Mercenaries ensued. Flaubert's novel *Salammbô* describes the mutual atrocities and repeated Berber desertions that ended in 237 BC when Hamilcar Barca seized the rebel leaders during negotiations and had their 40,000 men crushed to death by elephants.

Desperate for new sources of wealth, the Carthaginians turned to Spain. Within twenty years the Barcides succeeded in establishing there an influential kingdom. And from northern Spain, in the Second Punic War (218-201 BC), Hamilcar Barca's son Hannibal led his 59,000 men and 37 elephants famously over the Alps. Routing the Romans at Trasimenus, Trebia and Cannae, he came close to taking Rome but, after sixteen years in Italy, was brought back to Africa by Scipio's advances amongst the Berbers and finally defeated at Zama.

The Third Punic War is a pathetic story of forced suicide. For over half of the 2nd century BC, and with the help of the Berbers now relatively united under Massinissa, Rome held Carthage in submission. She was heavily taxed, made to surrender her warships and battle-elephants and internationally regarded as a vassal-state of Rome. She remained none the less a thorn in Rome's side, and in the Roman Senate Cato reiterated a call for destruction that Paquis, the French Lord Haw-Haw, was to take up in Nazi propaganda 2000 years later: 'England like Carthage shall be annihilated!'.

In 149 BC the Senate ordered the Carthaginians to abandon their city and move inland. Predictably they refused. The Romans besieged them for almost three years and, when Carthage finally fell, there took place a destruction so vicious that Dresden and Coventry pale beside it. Strabo wrote that there were 700,000 inside the walls when the siege began: 50,000 were alive, and enslaved, when it ended. For over ten days the starving Carthaginians were slowly forced back up Byrsa Hill. Each house became a battle-ground. As the hand-to-hand combat forced the occupants upstairs – there were often five or six storeys – the Romans demolished or set fire to the rooms below. Their general Scipio Aemilianus ordered pits to be dug, and the dead and wounded alike were thrown in to make way for his troops. After seven days of this the 50,000 survivors surrendered and were allowed to leave the burning city. The holocaust closed in on the Temple of Eshmun, atop the Hill of Byrsa, where King Hasdrubal was encircled with his family and the remnants of his people. As his men fell round him, the king brought his family out to ask Scipio for mercy. And his people turned against him. Shouting insults at the king, they set fire to the temple that sheltered them. The fighting then lulled for a moment. Hasdrubal's wife Sophonisbe thanked Scipio for his clemency, turned to her husband and cursed him as a coward and, taking their two children by the hand, walked back into the flames.

The fish, an early Christian symbol, still a popular motif of Tunisian filigree Carthage, the Antiquarium (left)

Colonnaded backdrop of the Roman theatre, Dougga (right)

Twin toilet at Bulla Regia

Roman. Scipio had every building in Carthage demolished, the land then ploughed over and sown with salt to make it barren, and a curse pronounced upon the site so that never again should it be inhabited. Not only in the 20th century are memories short. Twenty-four years later Caius Gracchus proposed a new city but, according to Plutarch, the Roman flag fell down and the sacrificial animals ran away in the storm that promptly followed. The Senate thought better of the suggestion. Only when the ex-Carthaginian territories had been reorganised and Utica made capital, when Massinissa's grand-nephew Jugurtha had been defeated, in 105 BC, and his Berber kingdom divided and ruled, and when Julius Caesar had routed the Pompeian army (and Juba's Berber camel-corps) at the Sahel battle of Thapsus in 46 BC, was Carthage rebuilt.

With the exception of the tophets, the ports and some uncertain masonry on Byrsa Hill, for example, the ruins we see today are all of the Roman Colonia Julia Karthago. Yet Carthage has left far less than other *municipia* and *coloniae*: Dougga, Bulla, Thuburbo Maius, Makthar, Haidra, Sbeitla and Gigthis are simply the best preserved or excavated. Everywhere there is evidence of intensive Roman settlement.

The advanced state of everything Roman in Tunisia is probably explained by its peacefulness. Once the Berber kings had been subdued and their land finally incorporated as Africa Nova, Tunisia was placed under direct Senate control, something done only with submissive territories. Caesar, then Augustus, settled there large numbers of out-of-work Italians, just as Mussolini was to do next door in Libya. The abundance of temples, not fortresses, is significant: while tiny Brittany kept four legions busy, the only military presence needed here was the single 'Third Legion Augusta', stationed far to the west at Tebessa.

Tunisia, with Egypt, became the 'granary of Rome'. Immigrant Italian landowners and Berber labourers supplied the empire with the wines and olives the Phoenicians had introduced. Nationwide highways were

El-Jem

constructed, which much of Tunisia's present network follows. The Romans, usually dry farmers, built aqueducts to supply their towns, incredible feats of engineering like the 50-odd miles of gently sloping pipe that run from Zaghouan to Carthage, high on arches over the valleys and in tunnels sheer through the hills. In many towns were baths bigger than our cinemas. Marble, locally from Chemtou or imported from Carrara, was commonplace builder's material. Quite modest villas had mosaics in such profusion that the Bardo Museum's collection today is indigestible.

With the Roman empire came Christianity. St Augustin, a Berber, was the Bishop of Hippone (Annaba) who presided over the Council of Carthage: for a time all 'Africa' was a diocese ministered from that city. But until their religion prevailed, African Christians had their share of persecution. The amphitheatres were the scenes of atrocities as horrible as in Rome (which Tunisia and Algeria kept supplied with lions, bears and other beasts). St Perpetua, a well-to-do housewife from Tebessa, was thrown to the animals on 7 March 203, in the Carthage amphitheatre near to which jazz concerts are now held each summer. St Felicity, a slave, was put in a cell beside the lions' when eight months pregnant. She delivered three days before being pulled apart in public.

It was largely Christianity that led to the collapse of Latin Tunisia. Christianity and the camel. For while the Catholic Church was rife with schisms, the orthodox attacking the Arian sect and the Donatists preaching revolt against orthodoxy, the spread of the camel in the Sahara (it was introduced much earlier) gave the Berbers a mobility that the Roman legions could not match. Weakened internally by religious and social unrest and externally by these southern raiders, Tunisia offered little resistance to the Vandals.

Sousse Museum. The noses of Roman busts in particular were literally vandalized.

Vandal and Byzantine.

As the Vandals inscribed, built and buried almost nothing, little is known about them. For concrete facts historians aver that the Vandals came in from Spain in the year 420. Or 428. Or perhaps 429. They took Carthage in 435. Or 439. And they were led by a king whose name was Genseric, or maybe Gaeseric, but who anyway had several wives and walked with a limp.

Exactly how much destruction the Vandals wreaked on Tunisia's cities, roads, ports and irrigation systems is another subject of academic uncertainty. They are believed even to have embellished Carthage with their plunder from Rome, and literal Vandalism explains the castration and removal of noses from Roman effigies everywhere. The Church's lists of bishoprics are the only detailed records of the time. From their showing elsewhere it is probably safe to assume that the Vandals contributed nothing of value to the country, save perhaps a few more genes in the Tunisian bloodstream. Within three generations the climate, plus the luxuries they had usurped, had tamed them to such an extent that when in AD 533 the Byzantine emperor Justinian sent 10,000 infantry and 6000 cavalry under Belisarius, to regain Tunisia for the Eastern Roman Empire, the Vandal king Gelimir was easily defeated: near Hammam-Lif and on the shores of Lake Sejoumi.

The Byzantines assumed the mantle of Rome, but it did not fit. They occupied the cities as far west as Haidra and south to Jerba, but built fortresses from the ashlars of villas, temples and baths. The development was symptomatic: harassed by the indigenous Berbers throughout their 140-year occupation, the Byzantines remained on the defensive.

Arab.

The rise of Islam, from the preaching of an unknown prophet to the possession of an empire that within 100 years stretched from Poitiers to Lahore, is a success-story no other religion can match. Promised a paradise of fragrant gardens, cool waters and dark-eyed houris if they died fighting the infidel, the Muslim warriors must have been formidable. Yet it was in Tunisia that these *mujahidin* met their first serious resistance.

In AD 647 Abdallah ibn Saad's first incursion reached Sbeitla, where the patrician-bishop Gregory had defied Byzantium by declaring independence the previous year. Having killed the patrician and amassed enormous plunder, the Arabs returned to Egypt, leaving Tunisia free but leaderless. A second raid took place in 665 but only in 668-670 did 150,000 Muslims, under Oqba ibn Nafi, invade and stay. They founded Kairouan, which was to be their base for the conquest of the West, the later Arab capital (Carthage was ignored) and the religious centre in modern times. Berber resistance continued, led first by Koseila (whose troops killed Oqba at Biskra), then at the end by an African Boadicea called El-Kahena (the feminine form of a word which, like Cohen, means Priest). The latter was killed and her army defeated in 702.

There was mass conversion of the Berbers to Islam. They joined the Arab army, and a Berber officer, Tariq, led the Muslim conquest of Spain in 711 with mostly Berber troops. They were for all that treated as second-class citizens, and consequent Berber dissatisfaction led to their secession as Kharijites, Islamic 'outsiders'. The egalitarian, puritanical sect survives on Jerba still. Kharijite Berbers took Kairouan in 745 and were in and out of what little power there was until 800.

In the year that saw Charlemagne crowned emperor on Christmas Day and Harun ar-Rashid sending him presents from Baghdad, an Arab governor named Ibrahim ibn El-Aghlab introduced what Tunisians consider

Monastir, the Aghlabite ribat of
Harthema

to be their Golden Age. Ibrahim quelled the dissident Kharijites and was
confirmed as emir by Harun ar-Rashid, his overlord in Baghdad. During
their 109 years in power his descendants, the Aghlabites, built fortified
medinas, as at Sfax; *ribats* (monastery-barracks) as at Monastir; great
mosques, the finest being Kairouan's, and waterworks of which only
the pools at Kairouan remain. They also pacified the country, conquered
Sicily in 827 and took back from Spain the idea of metal money. From their
capital of Kairouan, or more precisely nearby Rekada, envoys from Charlemagne and the Holy Roman Empire returned with glowing reports
of the Aghlabites' palaces, libraries and gardens – and of the crippling taxation imposed to pay for their drunkenness and sundry debaucheries.

The Catholic/Protestant equivalent in Islam is the schism between the
Sunnite and Shi'ite sects. The 'heretic' *Shi'a* claim their sectarian descent
from the Prophet's daughter Fatima – whence the Fatimites, who opposed
the excesses of the Aghlabites (none the less 'orthodox' Sunnites) and
evicted them from Kairouan in 909. The Fatimites' first Mahdi or 'Chosen
One', Caliph Ubaid-Allah ('Little Slave of God'), transferred the capital
to Mahdia. From here his descendants quashed the still-belligerent Berbers and proceeded to conquer a Tunisian empire that stretched from
Egypt in the east to the Atlantic in the west.

They left their empire of *Ifriqia* in the hands of their allies the Zirites
who, governing again from Kairouan, led the country through another
artistic, commercial and agricultural heyday. Schools and universities
flourished, overseas trade in Tunisian manufactures and farm-produce
ran high and the courts of the Zirite rulers were centres of refinement
that eclipsed those of their European contemporaries.

There follows the rare spectacle of a people sacrificing their prosperity
for their beliefs. In 1048 the Zirites repudiated the Fatimite caliphs in
Cairo and gave their allegiance to the Sunnite régime in Baghdad. They
did thereby escape Fatimite taxation, but this was not over-heavy: the
significance of the act lay in that the Zirites finally rejected the unorthodox, Shi'ite beliefs of the Fatimites.

They paid for it dearly. The Fatimite caliph El-Mustansir, having on his
hands two troublesome Arabian tribes called the Ben Hilal and the Sulaim,

sent them westward. These savage nomads destroyed villages, roads and irrigation systems, but could not build; carried off flocks and herds, but raised few themselves; burned and pillaged crops, but never farmed. Some 1700 years of intermittent but continual progress were undone within a decade.

With the Berbers held in check by the Hilalians, the Normans settled on Jerba in 1134. The Almohads, a Moroccan religious force, attacked Tunisia and the country became part of the Almohads' vast Mediterranean empire which, one writer says, their commander Abdul-Mumin 'won single-handed'. A Balearic troop then landed at Bougie and harassed Tunisia from the West. An Armenian bandit called Karakush did likewise from the east. The Tunisian Almohads, whose leader then was Nasser, succumbed on all fronts.

Seriousness was restored with the Hafsites. This dynasty, having declared itself independent of the Almohad governors, established itself in the new capital of Tunis. It was then, in 1236, that the small township the Phoenicians and Romans had called Tunes or Thines came to give its name to the country as a whole. The Almohads had already built a kasba, or citadel. The Hafsites enlarged this, as they did the medina (town), and encircled the latter with ramparts in the course of the 14th century. (They remained in power until 1574.) The expanding capital became more cosmopolitan. When the Christian *reconquista* of Spain ousted the Andalusians, these Muslim Huguenots settled in specially allotted streets and suburbs. When the European states started sending envoys and merchants to this key foreign city – Britain's first 'Agreement' dates from 1662 – quarters called funduqs were set aside for them.

The Hafsites' religious importance became such that the Sherif of Mecca, the Pope of Islam, acknowledged them as overlord in 1259. St Louis led a crusade against them eleven years later. He captured Carthage but was outnumbered by Tunis' army of 150,000. Having sent for reinforcements, he succumbed to the plague and died about 3 p.m. on 25 August 1270. His brother's army landed two hours later. Had it arrived one day sooner it might not have been able to prevent the French king's dying, but it might have helped smash the Hafsite nation and so change history.

Muslim versus the Infidel, in Tunisian painting on glass

Spanish. The Andalusians formed the skilled and civilized element of the population expelled from Spain. Their less cultured compatriots were the Corsairs. Initially to take revenge on the Christian invaders, these seafarers turned to piracy. Soon, as in so many human activities, financial gain obscured all other motives and piracy became big business.

Operating from bases like Tunis, Bizerta and Algiers, the maritime highwaymen used fast, light, well-armed craft against the slow and heavily laden merchant vessels. Important passengers were held for ransom, womenfolk raped then enslaved with the children, the crews usually killed. The merchantmen were looted and the onshore populations took ten per cent of the booty in return for 'fencing' and providing port facilities.

The Christian states often gave as good as they received. The Knights of St John were notorious, and by 1720 there were more than 10,000 slaves on Malta. The *bagnos* – a significantly Italian word for the human warehouses where the captives were stored awaiting sale or ransom – were as massive in Leghorn as they were in La Goulette.

In 1520 Charles V of Spain became Holy Roman Emperor and France enlisted against him the help of the Ottoman Turks. Tunisia became the scene of an early East-West struggle for power, a confrontation, mainly naval, between Muslim Turkey and Christian Spain. In 1534 the Corsair Khaireddin, youngest of the Barbarossa brothers, deposed the Hafsite Mulay Hassan, attacked and captured Bizerta, Tunis and La Goulette, marched inland to take Kairouan and joined forces with his brother Aruj, who already held Jerba. The Barbarossas, like their successor Dragut, were Muslim and backed by Turkey, so Charles V put to sea with 30,000 men. Contemporary German prints in the Bardo (studies for the massive canvases in Vienna's Kunsthistorisches Museum) graphically commemorate his capture of Tunis on 14 July 1535. In 1569 the Turkish Eulj Ali marched in from Algiers to retake the capital; in 1573 Don John of Austria countered successfully with a force of 20,000, but the Sublime Porte trumped in 1574, defeating the Spaniards and ousting the Hafsites.

Turkish. By 1574 all that was left of Spanish Tunisia was a series of impressive citadels along the coast, and a few more traits in the ethnic make-up. The Ottoman Turks, now directly from Constantinople, imposed their standard pattern of provincial control. And their comic-opera nomenclature. A *beylerbey* ruled from Algiers at first, but on his death in 1587 Tunisia, Libya and Algeria each became a regency governed by a *pasha* (and divided by boundaries that are the national frontiers today). The pasha came to accept joint rule with an army élite led by an aga. Junior officers – *deys* – mutinied in 1590 and one of their number, by joining forces with the *qabtan*, who directed the revenue from naval loot, and the *bey*, who enforced the equally ruthless extortion of taxes at home, rose to supreme power. Gradually the beys, the next tone down in the Turkish army scale, usurped it. One Murato Genovese, alias Murad, was in 1612 named pasha by the sultan in Constantinople and the accession in 1631 of his son Hamuda Pasha initiated a hereditary régime, but the lineage was cut short by an officers' plot in 1702. Hussein bin Ali, commander of the *spahis*, emerged on top – to install a dynasty that, as the Husseinites, survived until 1957.

Many of the early beys have the unusual reputation of being stalwart defenders of the faith, champions of material progress, and mass-murderers. The lucrative plunder of Christian ships was kept up; many of the country's most beautiful mosques, suqs and palaces were built at the beys' orders and expense; but large harems meant large families, with more and more sons

Tunis, the Tourbet of Hamuda Pasha

'Moorish' Tunis: Andalusian building styles brought back from Spain adopted and adapted by the Turks

and cousins to remove if one wished to simplify the succession. Bluebeards there certainly were – starting with the Barbarossas – but the majority of later beys seem to have been more effete than unduly libertine. Herbert Vivian, a Briton travelling in the 1890s, wrote: 'A visit to His Highness Ali, Bey of Tunis, is like a visit to an extinct volcano'. A number were beneficial to the old Tunisia (there were reforms in the mid-19th century under Mohammed Bey, Mohammed Sadoq Bey and the prestigious prime minister Kheireddine) but as the last of the line was illiterate, fluent only in Arabic and by then 80 years old, it is not surprising that on 27 July 1957 Tunisia's first independent parliament voted to abolish the monarchy *nem con*.

French. It was the beys' misdeeds in the 19th century that, with almost parable clarity, led to their undoing. In 1830 the French were installing themselves in Algeria and felt strong enough to frighten the bey next door into a treaty by which he renounced piracy. Inevitable bankruptcy made the régime dependent on long-term loans from French financiers, and gradually the stake in Tunisia's economy of interests such as the Oppenheimers' and Erlangers' gave them, like their British colleagues in Egypt, a say in its government. Corruption, however, continued to put their loans at risk. France and Britain had agreed to give each other a free hand in Tunisia and Cyprus respectively, and the new Kingdom of Italy had designs on Tunisia that were an open secret.

In the Khroumiria Mountains a traditional tribal pastime had been Raiding the Neighbours. The Algerian borderers were now, however, 'French-protected', so that when in 1880 a Tunisian clan crossed the frontier the French felt entitled to rush in. The French statesman Jules Ferry claimed that over 9000 Khroumiri fighters had invaded Algeria: the region's total population was then officially 7317. A 'small frontier force' was sent to defend the border: it consisted of 30,000 men in three armies, only one of which went to Khroumiria!

The French marched directly on Tunis and, having ensured that the pro-Italian Mohammed Sadoq Bey sign a 'Treaty of Protection', proceeded to quell by force the uprisings that broke out across the country. The treaties of Ksar Said (1881) and La Marsa (1883) obliged the bey to implement whatever reforms a French Resident Minister proposed. French officials moved into all spheres of administration. Large French concerns and individual *colons* sequestered the best farmlands, 'legally' by dispossessing Muslim farmers who could not produce title-deeds. French miners started to exploit the country's phosphates and rework its zinc-, lead- and iron-mines. Regiments of North African *tirailleurs* and *goums* were raised to fight in French armies overseas. Catholic churches and convent schools went up everywhere (even though Tunisia continued theoretically to owe allegiance to Muslim Turkey until 1919). Outside the medina the modern town of Tunis was built, as French in appearance and atmosphere as Gibraltar is British. Tunisia, technically only 'protected', was a thoroughgoing colony.

Beylical portrait in the Dar Chraiet Museum, Tozeur

Tunisia's first president, Habib Bourguiba, re-erected, equestrian, in La Goulette

Allied and Axis. Though France collapsed at the start of the Second World War, many Tunisians remained loyal and volunteered to fight with the Allies. Bourguiba, then an exiled 'revolutionary', was wooed by the Italians with promises of independence, but he and many of his colleagues declared themselves for the Allies even when the Axis had occupied their country.

The Allied landings in North Africa began on 8 November 1942. By then the German forces in Tunisia were increasing by 1000 men per day. The Race for Tunis had started. With Rommel defeated at El-Alamein four days earlier and Iraq and Syria occupied, the Allies hoped that the Axis stranglehold on the route to the East could be broken before the *Afrika* armies retreated intact to concentrate in Tunisia. On their defeat depended the landings in Italy. And on these, ultimately, D-Day.

The Race for Tunis was lost. The British and United States troops joined up with French units now in open resistance in the north, and 'Blade Force' was within 30 miles of the capital. But winter set in, the German build-up had been too efficient and the Allies, with inadequate communications and no forward airfields, were hard put to hold Mejez el-Bab and its infamous 'Long-Stop Hill'.

By the New Year of 1943, however, Montgomery was near. The Allies reorganized, with Eisenhower now Commander-in-Chief. The Germans advanced in a new offensive, well beyond the Pass of Kasserine, but the key towns of Beja, Mejez and Bou Arada stayed in Allied hands. In the south, Rommel was sick, but the Mareth Line hindered Montgomery's advance. He effectively overcame it in an operation almost as memorable as Hannibal's crossing of the Alps. Air attacks by the 'Tank Busters' enlarged the breach it succeeded in making. The New Zealanders, the Free French, the 4th Indian Division and the Gurkha Rifles followed up and by the end of March Montgomery had the 'impregnable' Mareth Line behind him. On 8 April, outside Gabes, Eighth Army units met up with American and First Army patrols from Tunisia's 'western front'.

The subsequent cornering of von Arnim's armies in the north-east made their resistance all the more intense, but their strongholds fell one by one (Takrouna to a heroic detachment of Maoris). Both Bizerta and Tunis were taken on 7 May 1943. From there the British 6th Armoured Division reached Hammamet, so cutting between the remaining German strongholds of Zaghouan and Cap Bon. The latter, where von Arnim had stock-piled

supplies and ammunition sufficient for a two-month siege, was not the scene of any last stand: the peninsula was secured, complete with dumps, by British patrols almost unopposed. The Germans and Italians were finally cornered on 11 May between Hammamet and Zaghouan, on the 12th the Indians captured von Arnim and on the 13th his successor surrendered with the Axis armies.

Tunisian. Unlike the Western Desert, the Tunisian countryside did not long remain littered with the debris of war. Already in 1944 the reinstated French authorities were salvaging derelict vehicles and weapons: not solely because of their value as scrap, more because their use by Tunisians threatened the French. For nationalism was growing. Bourguiba, now acknowledged leader of the Destour Party, was forced to seek asylum, first in Egypt. The next decade was to see him alternately overseas – canvasing support for the Tunisian cause at the United Nations, the Arab League and the capitals of Western Europe and south-east Asia – and under arrest. As his influence, even from prison, succeeded in conciliating official thinking in Paris, so the intransigence of Tunisia's French colony grew.

There followed a pattern of events familiar to British governments: the United Nations in 1952 approved a Latin-American resolution calling on the French to talk independence with Tunisia; the *fellagha* – Tunisian Mau Mau – began to attack outlying French farms; atrocities occurred. With general strikes and local embargoes on the colonists increasing, the latter replied in kind: their *Main Rouge* (Red Hand) organization machine-gunned the nationalist leaders Farhat Hached in Tunis on 5 December 1952 and Hedi Chaker in Nabeul on 13 September 1953. Metropolitan opinion and policy continued to wamble, but repression was the standard response. Thence the martyrs that every Tunisian town has named streets after and raised monuments to.

Things had reached Ulster extremes when Bourguiba was permitted to return. His arrival at La Goulette on 1 June 1955 was for Tunisians a combination of Mafeking and VE-Day; they celebrate it annually as Victory Day, although it was not until 20 March of the following year that Bourguiba seized the opportunity of a government change in France to negotiate independence.

The new republic, proclaimed on 25 July 1957, floundered through its first four years. It was denied French aid for helping the Algerian FLN. The French bombed Sakiet on 8 February 1958. There followed the Battle of Bizerta, with French troops finally leaving the base in October 1963. And in June 1964 the land held by Frenchmen, and some British Maltese, was nationalized.

For all that, Bourguiba increased his prestige internationally as the only head of a developing state to say Boo to de Gaulle. And to Nasser. Since the 1960s not only France again, but the USA, the UN, the World Bank, Germany, eastern Europe and now the Arab oil states have all stepped in with aid to Tunisia.

French-protectorate and modern Tunis, between the medina and the lake of El-Bahira

Museums

The Bardo. With probably the world's best display of mosaic and certainly North Africa's best Roman collection, the National Museum is well worth the short drive from Tunis.

The suburb of Le Bardo sprawls round its palace. The Hafsites first built here but little remains of the vast beylical complex that subsequently grew. In the 1860s Hesse-Wartegg found it 'a town of marble palaces . . . partly in the Renaissance, partly in the Oriental style' . . . with 'a true Eastern bazaar for the inhabitants . . . whose number amounts to two thousand' . . . and with sentries who 'crouch on the floor, knitting in hand'. The present palace, built in 1882 on the site that saw many centuries of the beys' wilful government and fleshly pleasures, now houses Parliament and the National Museum. The *Majlis el-Umma* (Council of the Nation) is the less imposing part to the left of the front portico of pink columns and white arches.

Beyond the archaeological shop are chambers of Punic stelae and earthenware from the tophets of Carthage and Sousse (8th-2nd century BC), with a case of terracotta masks, grinning, leering, ferocious or twisted and, opposite it, a side-room of Punic treasures. As a special favour the doorman may unlock and pull back the grille that guards an exquisite gold saddle-cover, Phoenician jewellery and toiletry trinkets, beads and seals in precious stone or bone, many of obvious Egyptian origin. The rest of the Punic rooms display bronzes, a beautiful alabaster urn, an ostrich's egg and oil-lamps – old men's heads with beards for wicks.

In the entrance hall are three jigsaw reconstructions from Korba, a wall of stelae and two remarkably preserved Punic sarcophagi in wood complete with contents. Beyond the stairs of the tiled Arab palace and the neo-Punic stelae of the Ghorfa, the Corridor of Stelae and Sarcophagi displays these, and funerary statues, in marble. At the end, the Thuburbo Maius Room's contents are disappointingly fragmentary.

In the Palaeo-Christian Room, the font, tomb covers and mosaics have

less sophistication but more impact: Daniel in the lions' den, builders at work and the Christian hall-marks of doves, grapes, labarum-signs and Dog Latin. Off this is the Bulla Regia Room: massive, exquisite statues of gods and emperors it must have been a joy to unearth (one Captain Benet had the privilege in 1906) and a 2nd-century mosaic of Perseus and Andromeda partly defaced but superb by any standard. The final room contains mostly curious but over-restored sphinxes and Egyptianized god-figures from Thinissut, near Hammamet.

The broad staircase up from the Christian Room is flanked by mosaics, many from Tabarka. On the upper floor, the inner area of mosaics is bordered by fifteen imposing Roman statues, with smaller busts in the cases and corners around. The ceiling of the Sousse Room, the former banqueting hall, splendidly complements its 'documentary' mosaics of Roman farm buildings and country-life scenes, cases of lamps, and the head and feet of a gigantic Jupiter (from Thuburbo Maius). Smaller rooms beyond display mosaics, seals and metalware from smaller Roman sites; a solid

silver platter is the only relic of antique Bizerta.

Across the patio from the entrance lies the former Music Room, with galleries, painted-wood ceiling and yet more mosaics. The dais at the end of the patio gives on to a perfect Tunisian chamber of tiled walls and sculpted-plaster cupolas, in which stands the famous 3rd-century mosaic of Virgil and the muses Clio and Melpomene (from Sousse), and adjoining which is the Prehistoric Room (flints, photographs and 'the world's first known monument of religious inspiration' . . . a pile of stones).

Far right: the Mahdia Rooms. In or about 81 BC a galley-load of Grecian treasures sank in a storm three miles off Mahdia. The wooden ship rotted but its bronze and stone cargo, half buried in the sea-bed, was spotted by a sponge-diver in 1907. It took until 1913 to raise this unique treasure trove (in metal, from 1500-lb anchors to bronze bed fittings and dwarf and hermaphrodite miniatures; in stone, from barnacle pock-marked capitals to still-shapely urns). Masterpiece of the array is the bronze duet of the allegorical Agon with the Hermes of Dionysos. Next the Oudna Room, the dining-room of the palace, with a fine painted ceiling and photo-plan of a Roman villa, plus Orpheus, Bacchus and a mosaic menagerie of elephants, bears, lions and other animals long since confined to sub-Saharan Africa.

On the next floor, room after room is floored and walled with mosaics depicting contemporary beasts and beliefs, and graphically – often heroically – recording Roman tastes, activities and life-styles. Beneath the gilded arches of this upper gallery, cases display lamps, stamps and seals; statues and brooches in bronze; vessels exquisite in irri-descent glass, and vases, masks, jugs, busts and statuettes in terra-cotta.

Beyond the Apollo at the head of the first stairs, the Arab Museum occupies a small beylical palace older (1831) than the main building which it adjoins: copperware, inlaid Dam-ascus-work, instruments, weapons, costumes and regional jewellery. Across the courtyard, with its spiral fluted columns, the T-shaped cham-ber is a traditional *qbu* (reception-room). Further Islamic exhibits (ceramic plaques, earthenware, glass objects, bookbindings and sculpted plasterwork) are on dis-play in a mezzanine room off the entrance-hall stairway and in chambers adjacent to the Thuburbo Maius Room.

Sousse Museum is installed
in its kasba, beside the city's light-house, the Tour Khalef. The main patio is gardened and attractive with mosaics: horses complete with bridle and rein; Neptune with fish, squids and octopus (also from Sousse). Be-tween them and in the next gallery is less sophisticated 3rd-5th century work, much with Christian anchors, doves, grapes, fish, labarum-signs, inverted swastikas and 'In Pace'. The long room off this gallery is impressive with almost 50 mosaics: from the vast end-piece of Nile-side hunting to the metre-square door-step mosaics of whippets and fish; from the realism of a saucy bacchant having his face slapped to the styl-ization of a fish-phallus entering Woman in the shape of a flirtatious eye. In the furthest gallery the 5th-6th-century tiles, all between ten and eleven inches square, decorated Christian basilicas with Adam and

Eve, beasts, and saints on horse-back. And off this, a room of Punic stelae from the tophet of Sousse, where by the 2nd century BC ani-mals were replacing the sacrificial infants . . . *Molchomor* instead of *Moloch*. Beyond, a gallery leads (right) into rooms of mosaics, am-phorae and terra-cotta tomb equip-ment – two 3rd-century BC Punic tombs even in situ below – and (ahead) to the gardens, toilets and rooms installed with painted frescoes and more fine mosaics: one a calender, another magnifi-cent with seven famous gladiators, named like their leopard antagon-ists, and between this and the Priapus headless but boastfully virile, a third (from Sousse; 3rd century AD) showing hartebeest, ostriches and oryx. There are steps up to the parapet and a panorama of the medina. As you return, the fourth gallery of the main courtyard contains a mosaic peacock in full tail, a grotesque tragic mask and mosaic floors *passim*.

Nereid and dolphins in Roman mosaic

The Museum of El-Jem is
a typical Roman villa in design: the vestibule precedes a colonnad-ed patio, its mosaics intact but un-imaginative. Of the rooms off, that to the left was hedonistic with mos-aic miniatures of Bacchanalians and beasts, Alpheus seducing Arethusa, Apollo pursuing Daphne and other *amours divines* . . . until prudish officialdom replaced them with crude cement. The same fate has befallen the magnificent lions and tigers graphically attacking wild boar and asses. Of the several 'Four Seasons' surviving in the room ahead, one is surrounded by swastikas; another masterpiece apt-ly depicts the Nine Muses. The far gallery is varied with cases of bronze coins and household implements. In the villas excavated behind the museum's extension, one mosaic invokes a blessing on the name of the occupant. Another, not the best preserved but probably unique, shows Christian victims being held by gladiators and torn apart by panthers, the blood running down in square mosaic drops.

Around Tunisia today

Tunis, whether approached by sea or air, makes an exceptional first impression. Landfall, by ferry, is the russet cliffs of Carthage, the hills of Byrsa and 'Sidi Bou' and, hazy to the south, the Cap Bon peninsula like arms outstretched in welcome. Then Bou Kornine looming closer and the coastline slowly crystallizing as the first suburbs of Tunis, the 'Prophet's white Burnus'. Flying, on a clear day, brings a distant glimpse of the lakes behind Bizerta, the precipitous headland of Raf-Raf and the rock-island Pilao, Ghar el-Melh's strange lagoon, the sebkha-flats of Raouad, and finally low over the shallow Lake of Tunis which, uniquely cleft by dyke and canal, makes the capital's 'flight path' scenic, safe and very central.

With an out-of-town motorway and cloverleaf flyovers, a *métro léger* tramway recently completed,

good hotels, restaurants and near-by beaches, modern stadiums and excellent museums, a population of more than a million, a university older than Oxford's, the Arab League headquarters and even a well-stocked zoo, Tunis is a pleasantly pulsating place. And within it lies a mediaeval town which, with its close-packed alleys of mosques, suqs, zawias, arches and mashrabias, belongs to another civilization.

The Avenue Habib Bourguiba and Lake of Tunis (left)
The Cathedral of St Vincent de Paul, and in the Central Market (lower left)
The Place du 7 novembre 1987; in the Jellaz; the Belvedere Gardens (below)

The Place du Gouvernement lies, in the upper reaches of the medina, below the site of the capital's kasba. The Hafsites first erected a 13th-15th-century palace here; the Turks extended this into a citadel, and the French razed every-thing in the 1950s. Below the Aziza Othmana Hospital and the Shrine of Sidi Laz, ministries surround 'Govern-ment Square': that on the far side with one face of its clock-tower an erratic Arabic date-clock, and two curious Arabic zodiacs inscribed in its façade; the near side occupied by the Dar el-Bey ('House of the Bey'). Built in the 18th century, it in 1816 accommodated the then Princess of Wales ('Prinny's' footloose and ill-fated wife, Caroline).

The main street of Tunis, the Avenue Jules-Ferry before independence, is now, like every Tunisian main street, named Avenue Habib Bourguiba. Precisely one mile long, it runs from the edge of the lake called El-Bahira (the Little Sea) almost to the medina entrance known as Bab el-Bahar (the Sea Gate). For the salt waters of El-Bahira once covered this area right up to the walls of the medina. One Baroness Fasciotti, so the story goes, extended her lakeside property by paying the local dustmen to dump their cart-loads in the shallows.

43

The Porte de France, or Bab el-Bahar, forms the watershed between the old and new Tunis. The Hafsites' walls have mostly been demolished and the 'Sea Gate' now stands isolated, unchanged since 1848 until it received, in 1985, the fine restoration it both needed and deserved, plus a decorous surround of pink and buff paving. Prior to independence, the arch half-concealed an oblique bronze statue of Cardinal Lavigerie, Tunisia's first White Father. The British Embassy and the excellent British Council library occupy the most prominent corner of this Place de la Victoire. To the left, the Rue de la Commission boasts Garibaldi's pied-à-terre. Ancient Tunis was encircled by two lines of ramparts of which only the inner ring now survives in the Bab el-Bahar and the Bab el-Jedid ('Newgate').

The Central Market, the locals' 'Fondouk el-Ghalla', is a Billingsgate hall smelly with fish and a vast and colourful Covent Garden courtyard. The alleys between them sell (to one side) meat, cheese, snails and Tuniso-Sicilian spices and (to the other) live rabbits, turkeys and pigeons, while boys sit plucking and gutting chickens, decapitated to order.

The Central Market, Tunis

Tunis, the Bab el-Bahar and Place de la Victoire

Tunis Medina.

In Tunis is the largest and best-maintained example of the medinas seen also in Hammamet, Kairouan, Sfax, Sousse, Monastir and Mahdia. The word in Arabic means nothing more than 'town' (French-speaking Tunisians prefer in fact 'la Ville arabe') – the once high-walled, still narrow-alley-ed burghs that mediaeval travellers hurried to reach before the mass-ive gate (*bab*) closed safe against intruders for the night. Tunisian styles of building and living are at their most typical in the medinas, and a word about them here will save repetition.

Suq is 'market' and spelt incor-rectly *souk* in French transliter-ations. Suqs and side-streets are narrow for defence against in-vaders in the days before machine-guns; some still have double doors to seal them off completely at each end. Islam likes elaborate doorways: in Tunisia the surrounds are usually sculpted sandstone and the doors themselves black-studded and painted blue, green or occasionally ochre. Door-knockers generally are a woman's hand (the lucky *main de Fatma*) albeit lace-cuffed, clasped round a ball and often in black iron. Over upper windows the pictures-que half-fig of wrought iron is the *mashrabia*, the 'blind' of an embras-ure from which once-cloistered wives could see and not be seen.

Islam's place of worship is, of course, the mosque (*masjid* or *jami'*), often named after a patron saint or founder. From the minaret (*soma'a*) the faithful are called to prayer five times a day. This they do in the prayer-room, or sometimes in summer in the courtyard outside, having first drawn water from the marble-rimmed well or visited the adjacent *midha* (toilet) for the ritual ablution of private parts and arms up to the elbow.

The mosque's founder will often be buried in a mausoleum (*tourbet*) beside or near the mosque. Outside the towns each community has a holy man or two (*marabout*) who is similarly inhumed in a square, white-domed shrine also called marabout. The numerousness of Tunisia's mar-abouts (every village has its Sidi This or Sidi That and in Tunis they are legion) should not be seen as indicating any excess of saintliness. Qoranic erudition, undocumented miracles or just curing ailing babies may entitle certain marabouts to fame and a sizeable following, but with others the sphere of influence goes little further than friends and family who, according to their means, build his final resting place.

The *zawia* is a less ostentatious tourbet, 'a place where one comes to rest and reflect, on the tomb of a saint or at the cenotaph of another saint buried elsewhere', according to Monsieur Zbiss' *Monuments de Tunis*. In tourbets, zawias and marabouts the body lies beneath a paving-stone which is sometimes simply inscribed, sometimes adorn-ed with a turban-shaped headstone, but more frequently covered with a large green 'coffin' (albeit empty) decked with red, white or green silk banners. Women especially believe fervently in a favourite saint and pay frequent visits to light decorated candles in his shrine.

The *medersa* is a college hostel where, like Oxford's undergrad-uates, the students of the Zituna University lived in chambers off a rectangular, colonnaded court. Un-less maintained by the State, most of these edifices, exquisite with sculp-ted-plaster cupolas and ceramic-tiled walls, now house poor families that hang their washing between the ancient columns and live off the baksheesh of visitors and pilgrims.

Some suqs may be painted now brighter than new, others may be fading, but in essence neither they nor the way of life within them has changed for seven centuries. Merchants still work in the antique booths, they walk across cobbles that their ancestors trod to pray in the selfsame mosques. If touts still pester with their cheap souvenirs, remember they were doing no differently half a millennium ago. Children were playing the same games in these alleys when England ruled France.

Tunis Medina, the Shrine of Sidi Mahrez

The Rue Jamaa ez-Zitouna rises from the Bab el-Bahar between open-fronted shops which, if the suqs were still named after their trades as once they were, would make this the Suq of Souvenirs. At number 12, municipal offices now occupy the former Church of the Holy Cross, the capital's second Christian place of worship, founded in 1662 by an early French chaplain to the European community. For this, the quarter of alleys between the British Embassy and the Zituna Mosque, was the first funduq.

The Great Mosque or Mosque of the Olive-tree (*Jami' ez-Zituna*) is the largest and oldest in Tunis, and second in Tunisia only to Kairouan's. It was started by the Umayyad rulers in 732, completed by the Aghlabites in 864, enlarged by the Zirites in the 10th century and again by the Turks in 1637. The ceiling was replaced in 1782 and the whole structure restored between 1962 and 1975. Not so virtuoso as Kairouan's, the prayer-room is perhaps a more convincing monument to Islam: antique capitals on the coppice of columns; huge chandeliers of Venetian glass; cases of ancient manuscripts, some illuminated, by the south wall; the mihrab a sculpted masterpiece showing, not quite exactly, the direction of Mecca, and in front of it the superbly sculpted cupola, the Zirites' contribution.

The 13th-century Suq el-Attarine (the Perfumers) is one of the most beautiful. Low narrow shops, all green and gold, sell henna and sundry herbs for perfumes, their ceilings often stalactitic with candles in pink, white or gold, some plain, some worked in silver for marabouts' shrines or wedding-feasts, and the shelves amber, orange and pink with jars of incense and heavy perfumes.

Tunis Medina, the Rue Jamaa ez-Zitouna

Perfumer in the Suq el-Attarine

The so-called Palais d'Orient is the roof of a large bazaar situated in the Suq el-Leffa. As an Oriental Palace it is phoney – the tiled arches and walls are a recent setting for the older fragments of masonry – but it was the first of the several tourist *terrasses* and offers a fine panorama of the city's skyline.

The Souk et-Trouk (Suq of the Turks) was designed by Yusef Dey in 1630 as the city's finest thoroughfare: its reputation with visitors today centres on the M'rabet, a restaurant of which the ground floor is a lofty, solemn café named after the marabouts interred along one side.

The vaulted Rue du Château adjoins the El-Ksar Mosque, constructed in 1106, conspicuous with its square minaret added in 1674, and extensively refaced in 1978-79. The mosque was founded by the 11th-12th-century Beni Khorasan, who came to control the Tunis district after the Hilalian invasion had put an end to all central authority.

The Mosque of Hamuda Pasha was built in 1654 and served as model for the Habib Bourguiba Mosque in Monastir. Steps lead into the courtyard with the elegant octagonal minaret and, to the right, Hamuda Pasha's tourbet (also added in 1655). Black-and-white blind arches, pink columns, green roof-tiles and gold crescent moons give the mausoleum an almost Baroque appearance.

Tunis Medina, the Rue du Château

The M'rabet, 'Suq of the Turks'

The mausoleum (tourbet) of Hamuda Pasha

The Tomb of Princess Aziza Othmana occupies the Medersat Echemmahia, built in the 13th century and rebuilt in 1647. Othman Dey's daughter Fatima, who died the year before, may have been famous for her charity – whence *Aziza* (Beloved) – but the two ornate qubbas of 24 tombs were in 1979 restored rather parsimoniously.

The Tourbet of Sidi Mahrez, dating from 1862, enshrines Abu Mohammed Mahrez es-Sadiqi, the patron 'saint' of Tunis who, after enemy ravages in 944, inspired the Tunisians to rally and rebuild the town. Now Tunis women actually queue, some in sifsaris, some in jeans and dark glasses, to draw washing water from the well in the domed ante-room, slip off their shoes and pray at the marabout's ornately caged tomb. Opposite the shrine stands the Sidi Mahrez Mosque (1675-92, restored 1970-72), its domes reminiscent of Istanbul.

Carthage is rather a commuters' suburb now, with the ancient sites respectably in place amidst the bourgeois villas. In 1835 Grenville Temple wrote in his *Excursions in the Mediterranean*: 'All vestiges of the splendour and magnificence of the mighty city had indeed past away . . . I beheld nothing more than a few scattered and shapeless masses of masonry . . . My heart sank within me'. Modern visitors, if less elegiacally, often share his feelings. Scipio obliterated the Punic capital and after more than a millennium of Muslim neglect came the more destructive pillage of the Age of Enlightenment. (A British consul had much of Dougga's mausoleum pulled down in 1842 to remove the dedicatory Libyco-Punic plaque, and the crew of a 19th-century British warship was sent ashore at Carthage with orders to lade chunks of the Baths of Antoninus.) It was

therefore regrettable but wise that this century's archaeological authorities should have stripped as much as they possibly could from their antique sites, to safeguard their heirlooms in museum vaults and so prevent their ending up as part of a peasant's sheep-pen or the décor of some foreigner's home. Habib Bourguiba had in fact been quoted as saying that, if ever Tunisia struck oil wealth, the bourgeois villas would all be removed and Carthage restored. Bourguiba has since been removed – and the villas remain – but UNESCO in 1972 launched an 'unprecedented rescue operation' to 'safeguard' this capital of the ancient world. Teams of archaeologists from Britain, North America and several European states worked beside Tunisians for some ten seasons to excavate and document several of the few remaining 'undeveloped' sites.

The tophet is indicated 'Sanctuaire punique'. Here stood the temples of Tanit and Baal Hammon who demanded human sacrifice. To the right of the entrance gape the ugly pits where the children's ashes were discovered in 1921 and exhumed in 1942-43. So many four-twelve year-olds were strangled then burned in the course of 600 years that the urns with their ashes filled the allotted area; fresh layers of urns and steles were therefore laid on top. Steles are the commemorative headstones, varying in style through the centuries, that now crowd the area left of the entrance.

Carthage, the Punic Ports

Carthage, the Baths of Antoninus

The Punic Ports stretch along the shore beyond the tophet. The nearer of these placid village-ponds was the mercantile port, the more northerly a larger *cothon* for the Punic navy. With its colonnaded dry docks for 220 vessels, the latter was the pride of Carthage's sea-power; from here its ships sailed to the ends of the then-known world. The site with its central Island of the Admiralty was allocated in 1975 to the British partici-pants in the 'Save Carthage' project, who excavated one of the original 30 shipsheds, plus later Roman remains. In the Antiquarium two reconstructions depict respectively the Punic port of 150 BC and its Roman successor of AD 200. They are not fanciful, as the layman might suspect, but 'the best recon-struction archaeologists can make from the evidence recovered in the excavations'.

The Baths of Antoninus Pius were begun by the emperor Hadrian (AD 117-138) and completed by his successor Antonin-us Pius (138-161). Most of the impressive nine acres of masonry form merely the basement , the 'works' of the baths, with stores of wood for the furnaces and earthenware pipes for the hot water they supplied. The actual baths – from hot *caldarium* through *tepidarium* to *frigidarium*, one part for women, one for men – were on an upper floor level with the present boundary track. Their ceiling was supported by twelve fluted and grey granite columns, and one Corinthian capital alone has been found weighing some four tons. (Since 1985 it no longer adorns the nearby cross-roads – where a replica has replaced it – but crowns the 'grand column' resurrected in the baths.) It was all this that came crashing through the basement roof, at a date unknown, to leave the tremendous vestiges visible today.

The Antiquarium is reached by steep and well-paved Roman streets that climb between the house-walls, cisterns and columns of the 'Parc Archéologique des Villas Romaines'. Laid out in 1961 with a panoramic terrace of column stumps, mosaics, cannon balls and capitals, in-scribed plinths, well-heads and shapely marble busts, the Antiquarium museum was closed in 1981 and replaced by a semicircular 'Roman orchestra' and a very Tuscan patio of pink columns, paving and pergola.

Sidi Bou Said

Sidi Bou Said.

Whenever brochures show a 'typical Tunisian village' of cobbled streets, white walls, studded blue doors and black mashrabias, it is probably 'Sidi Bou'. Rather like an oriental Clovelly, it winds round the top of a hill which became a beacon for early navigators and a haven for this century's artists, writers and affluent gentlefolk. A Muslim legend has it that St Louis did not die on Byrsa Hill but took French leave of his army, married a Berber girl and became the local saint Bou Said (known for curing rheumatism and stopping scorpions from stinging). As, however, St Louis did not arrive until 1270 and the historical Abu Said Khalifa bin Yahia et-Temimi el-Baji died in 1231, we have here another Dido-and-Aeneas anachronism.

Today's influx of Westerners, whether trippers or settlers, is something of a historical irony. Atop the ancient Cape Carthage, where the Punic suburb of Megara spread, Muslims of the Middle Ages built a ribat from which to defend the coast against Christian raiders. St Louis died in the shadow of this stronghold of early Sufism, Islamic mysticism. The Corsairs made 'Sidi Bou' their mascot, the patron of anti-Christian piracy, and although Charles V, from 1535 to 1574, maintained here a Spanish garrison (which included Cervantes, pre-*Don Quixote*), Christians until 1820 were actually forbidden to enter the picturesque village. Nowadays picturesqueness is the village's prime concern: the French buried cables and telephone lines and the present municipality keeps up the good work by fining householders who do not whitewash annually or paint doors blue. Visitors now, Muslim or not, wander unrestricted: up past the 'museum', in fact the municipal art gallery, to the much-vaunted Café des Nattes for the almost mandatory cup of mint tea on the mat-covered seats, then past the shop selling sticky bambaloni cakes to the Shrine of Sidi Bou Said, once a sanctuary for criminals.

Utica. The history of Outih, the first known Phoenician settlement in Tunisia, provides in many ways a counterpoint to that of Carthage. Utica, according to Pliny the Elder, was founded by trader-sailors from Tyre on a prehistoric site in 1101 BC. Thus Carthage's senior by some 300 years, the northern city maintained its independence of the Punic capital for a further 300 years, being forced into allegiance in the 5th century BC. Agathocles, who failed to take Carthage, captured Utica in 308 BC. After the First Punic War, the rebel mercenaries found refuge here, and Hamilcar Barca's consequent reduction of Utica was curiously vindicated in the Third Punic War, when the town not only refused to assist Carthage but even served as Rome's operational base against the sister-city – thereby escaping the fate that Scipio inflicted on the capital and its allies, Punic Bizerta, Kelibia and Nabeul.

As a further Roman 'reward', Utica was first made a free city, in 144 BC, then capital of the *provincia Africa*. Marius landed here with his legions to put down Jugurtha in 107 BC, and in 49-45 the Pompeian resistance to Caesar in Africa was maintained by 'Cato Uticensis'. Great-grandson of the Cato who so famously inveighed against Carthage, he stabbed himself, at Utica, after Caesar's final triumph at Thapsus. Though Utica continued to prosper in the 2nd and 3rd centuries AD, it was probably this Pompeian association that prompted Caesar to have Carthage resurrected.

None of this, however, can be seen or even conjectured from the present-day remains, which were excavated first in 1905 but most in 1948-58. Of the various edifices 'identified' by their main features – the 'House of the Treasure', 'of the Hunt', 'of the Capitals' – only the House of the Fountain is of

any great interest: an arch with neat sockets for the roof-beams and bolts; three boarded, well-preserved mosaics with scenes of fishermen and fish; rooms off with mosaic and marble floors in pink, green, cream and grey, and the lead piping broken illustratively open in places.

Over the hill behind the *ghourbi*-huts are the scattered ruins of what might have been a theatre and, above the causeway that runs Hobbema-esque to the horizon, a smaller Punic cemetery.

Beyond the dip below the main necropolis, further excavation has exposed the walls of (perhaps) a hilltop fort; a forum area of column stumps and paving; a putative temple; a rectangular pool with basins and baths; floors in marble and geometric mosaic, and walls in the attractive criss-cross pattern known as *opus reticulatum* and also seen at Bulla Regia.

Porto Farina, beside its lagoon, is known locally as Unq el-Jemel (Camel's Neck) and officially as Ghar el-Melh (the Cave – or Hole – of Salt). The name of Rusucmona is all that remains of this original outpost of Punic Utica. Some Roman vestiges, then 1200 years of historical somnolence rudely cut short first by Charles V, who sheltered and watered his fleet here before the raid on La Goulette, and by Admiral Blake, who bombarded the port in 1654 when Hamuda Pasha refused to release English captives. In 1837 Ahmed Bey began a grandiose project of palaces and barracks in this port the Corsairs had made famous. The three fortresses they built became prisons; only in 1965 were the last of the inmates transferred to Bizerta. Today, with the twelve-square-mile anchorage ruined by the Mejerda's silt, Ghar el-Melh is known for its potatoes, and its veiled women.

The road in winds through tight market-gardens and past the first fort: massive bastions, an impressive moat and Ghazi Sultan Mohammed honoured as builder in the dedicatory plaque. It narrows through an arcade of booths, continues between the Martyrs' Memorial and the second fortress/prison/college, and curves past the third ex-prison, down to the abandoned shipsheds and battlemented mole of the photogenic port.

Bizerta. Until 1963 the French were in jealous possession of this former Corsair haven; the risorgimento feared it as 'a pistol levelled at the heart of Italy'; it was a key operational base, bitterly contested, of World War II, and the first NATO generals considered it vital to Western defence. But nuclear thinking, supertankers and a closed Suez Canal made Bizerta redundant. At the 'back' of the lake the vast arsenal of Ferryville (now Menzel Bourguiba) has been partly converted into factories. Although something stark and military still stands on most hilltops around, the town today is more quaint than strategic.

The Vieux Port separates the new town from the old. It is difficult to imagine how, until 1890, the Old Port was part of the original canal through to the lake. In the canal was an island, since reattached to become the quay on which now stand shops and cafés.

The kasba you enter by a vaulted passage, bent to hamper mediaeval invaders. The 17th-century Mosque of the Medina confronts you, its minaret retiled but its interest minimal. The medina beyond is narrow alleys, often arched, and neat discreet homes, a pretty pastel wash on every wall. Inside the gate, steps lead up to the reworked battlements: on the broad rampart walk, five assorted cannon guard the headland.

The hilltop behind is crowned by the Fort of Spain, where the bastioned walls converge. Also known as the Fort of Sidi Salem, the citadel was built by the Turks in 1573 and reworked by Yusef Dey in 1620-42, to be transformed in 1968 into a starkly attractive open-air theatre. The ramparts offer good views (to the south) of the town, backed everlastingly by the distant flame of Bizerta's refinery-flare, and below, towards the sea, of the cemetery of Sidi Bou Hadid (with, as always, one gravestone for men, two for women).

Tabarka, scenically, is difficult to fault: the mountains of Khroumiria step back from the beaches to leave room for the compact town. The sands stretch round a sheltered bay, giving way in places to rocky promontories. A pretty island-cone off shore is topped by a castle to complete the picturesqueness.

If Tabarka has waited 2000 years for its promotion from port to resort, there is good historical reason. After Carthage the Phoenicians founded Thabraca (Bushy Place) and the subsequent Roman port handled not only 'Numidian' marble from Chemtou but also the cork, leather, timber and minerals of Khroumiria. The town's Christian connections we know from the Bardo's mosaics. Its coral attracted the Genoese families of Lomellini and Grimaldi who, the story goes, had Charles V swap the captured Corsair Dragut for the island of 'Tabarque' in 1542. As a Christian outpost the island numbered some 1200 inhabitants when, in 1741, Ali Pasha Bey cut

short the Franco-Genoese wrangle over who owned Tabarka by sending his son to take it and sell them as slaves. Razing the 'imposing ruins of an immense edifice' (the Roman baths) in order to build the town square, burying Punic and Roman remains beneath their styleless streets, the French 'urbanized' in the 1900s. Blissfully unaware of this archaeological sacrilege, their young compatriots now contribute most to Tabarka's summer popularity.

The Aiguilles (Needles) are fantastically eroded, 60-foot stacks that punctuate the coast close to the town centre. The island of Tabarka (600 yards long, 400 wide and 70 high) was attached to the mainland in 1952 by means of a 400-yard mole, and a leisurely track winds up to the Genoese fort and the lighthouse. Despite its 5000 candle-power mantle and a range of eighteen sea-miles, the flashing-light could not prevent the wrecking of the French *Auvergne* in 1876 and *Diane* in 1922. Relics of the latter, so they say, can still be seen off the Morjane beach.

The island, castle and bay of Tabarka, seen from the Algeria road

Tabarka, the Aiguilles

Bulla Regia.

If the ruins, at first sight, do not impress with the grandeur of Dougga or Thuburbo, it is partly because the town that the Romans established on a Numidian site was destroyed by earthquake and partly because its palatial villas were mostly built underground. 'Regia' because of the 'royal' residence here of one of Massinissa's 50-odd sons.

The main site is entered via the Baths of Julia Memmia. Excavated partially in 1909-24, this 2nd-century edifice is impressive with mosaics, arches and high-vaulted walls, intact or restored, in the main halls and side-rooms. The tapered tubes still visible in the vaulting of the first chambers were used to shape the quick-drying plaster. From the fine north-west façade, stairs climb to a well-paved road.

Opposite, steps and a track lead up past a sunken villa, inconspicuous basilicas and the 'House of the Treasure', in the last of which a staircase descends to a floor of fine tesserae but unexciting design. The track up-hill becomes a paved Roman lane climbing first to the House of the Peacock (each edifice is named from the finest mosaic found in it) and to the House of the Hunt, recognizable by its reddish columns. This is the most remarkable of Bulla Regia's underground mansions: a colonnade surrounds the *atrium* (courtyard) and, in the rooms off, there are mosaics even on the platforms raised for beds. The kitchen is recognized by its smoke-stained walls, the vaulted *oecus* (dining-room) by its 'culinary' mosaics and its cistern. Excavations here in 1973 revealed the 'Maison de la nouvelle Chasse' adjoining: the namesake mosaic (covered protectively in sand) depicts hunters on foot and on horseback, lions and half a spitted hog. The next complex of walls, stumpy columns and fine fish-and-fowl mosaics is a temple, to judge by the mosaic inscription '*hecdomvsdei*', 'This (is) the house of God'. The street-level area of the adjacent 'Fishing House' is an astonishing series of rock-rimmed vents for the ducts that descend to a less elaborate atrium and 'cloister'-rooms below. On the paved lane running north beside this 'Maison de la Pêche', the first intact mosaic floor indicates the so-called House of Amphitrite: her head an exquisite mosaic on a background of black tesserae and, in the main triclinium, the same face on a nude body astride a headless creature with wings for forelegs and hind-legs back-to-front. Below the Fishing House, the Temple of Apollo (Bulla's patron) lies to the left of the grassy forum, from which steps continue down to the market area. The clover-leaf bath here, beautiful with mosaic, was reserved for the actors of the theatre ahead. Similar to Dougga's (save that here, as at Kasserine, many balustrades remain in place), it is equally evocative. Eight aisles (*vomitoria*) divide the eleven rows of seats (*cavea*). The orchestra, with a mosaic circus bear, precedes the *proscenium* (stage). A well-paved lane then leads west between the Temple of Isis and, to the south, an unusual Roman feature: two long public esplanades accompanied by ornamental 'moats'. Straight on beyond the baths the lane stops before the insignificant Byzantine fortress, from which a wider and even better road runs down to the seven cisterns and a building of unknown purpose but remarkable design, the criss-cross *opus reticulatum* of Italian inspiration.

Hammamet's uniqueness can best be appreciated from the hills around. The balding slopes close in on Nabeul to the north. Behind the curve of the perfect bay is one long swath of citrus green that fades southwards into the sebkha. The sheen of the olive- and orange-groves is flecked with the white of occasional villas. Solemn lines of cypresses add dignity. Sisal 'sticks' and angular wind-pumps spike the horizon, the classic grotesque contrast in this suave countryside.

It is easy to see why hoteliers followed the foreign artists and aesthetes who in the 1920s settled here. And why the Romans preceded them en masse. From the colonia promoted in AD 179 by a local proconsul, Salvius Julianus, there remains a little-known 'dig' on the beach. The Roman place-name of Putput, Pudput or Pupput was changed by the Arabs to Hammamet, meaning variously 'bathing-places' or 'doves'.

Historical mentions are thereafter intermittent. Strategically prominent between two sheltered bays, the headland was first fortified in 904. Invasion by the Normans, occupation by the Hafsites and the Spanish-Corsair confrontation all meant for Hammamet the usual sieges, battles and bloodshed. Seized by Dragut in 1560, blockaded in vain by Andrea Doria, the garrison was the victim of a Trojan-horse trick in 1602, when 300 Knights of Malta landed disguised as fellow Muslims. They approached playing Arab pipe and drums, were welcomed with open arms and promptly sacked the town. When ten galleons from Sicily and Malta were sighted in 1605, the Muslim inhabitants fled: then turned the historical tables by sending back 100 men unseen to decimate the 1100 invaders.

Become in consequence notorious in Europe (as 'Mahometta' or 'La Mahomette'), Hammamet played a small part in Tunisia's first civil war. Leading a revolt against Bey Murad I, a dey known as Hajj Ali Laz retreated here in 1673, to be killed and buried in the kasba. In 1881, when the French marched in, the townspeople helped repel a first column at El-Arba'in. Though superior forces were soon sent to impose French rule, Hammamet won a tiny final victory in its typically seductive way: the French commanding officer, Captain Bordier, became so enamoured of the place that he resigned his commission and retired to settle here.

The French built roads and a railway and introduced the telephone. In the Gay Twenties people of means settled into a less brittle life of white villas, antique gardens and warm sands. The Rumanian George Sebastian built what Frank Lloyd Wright called 'the most beautiful house I know'. The War interrupted things but left little mark: the Foreign Legion garrisoned the kasba, a Senegalese regiment was stationed near by, a couple of bunkers were built on the beach, and the Germans – unlike André Gide and Paul Klee, who were invited – installed themselves at Sebastian's. Apart from clandestine activity against the French protectorate, and open bloody conflict in 1952, the history of Hammamet since is tourism pure and simple.

Mornings in Hammamet, mending the nets

The medina is Hammamet's only real landmark. Lapped on one side by the sea, its walls back on to the headland cemetery and face the sweep of beach that, colourful with fishing-boats, curves south to the hotels. The ramparts, repeatedly restored, were first erected in 904 by the Aghlabite emir Ibrahim II. But their present parallelogram-shape and size – roughly 300 by 100 yards – are usually attributed to the Hafsite ruler Abu Zakaria who, building the Great Mosque in 1236, wanted to protect it. Of the three original doors, the Bab es-Suq (Market Gate) is open to infidels since 1881. It bends – a mediaeval means of defence – into the one street of the suq. Opposite the Turkish bath stands the Great Mosque. To Abu Zakaria's original, his successor Abu Amr Othman added the minaret in the late 15th century. It was refaced in 1972, the whole edifice being reworked both by Bey Hassine in 1727 and by the municipality in 1978-79.

The kasba is reached either via the suq or by the original Sea Gate, the Bab el-Bahar, which every visiting photographer discovers as a photogenic frame to the fishing-boats and bay. From the *place* ahead, where the suq ends, a lane of jazzy shops runs under the walls to the Marabout of Sidi Bou Hadid. (Its conversion into café is not sacrilege: sipping mint tea and smoking hubble-bubbles on tombs is, as in Tunis' M'rabet Restaurant, an accepted Tunisian tradition.)

Steep steps lead up into the kasba itself. Restored in 1977-79, the courtyard shelters trees, three undated and un-mounted cannon, and the Marabout of Sidi Bou Ali (a standard *qubba*-dome with a sunken, flag-draped catafalque). Beside the cannon, steps climb again to the *Chemin de Ronde*, the rampart walk. The Moorish café installed in 1978 is neat, clean and friendly, the panorama splendid of the old town and the bay.

The International Cultural Centre has been installed in George Sebastian's incomparable house. Cypress-trees and white colonnades surround the cool tiled pool; a refectory table is of black monolithic marble; bedrooms have fitted antique mirrors and sunken Roman baths. Each summer the 22 acres of park become public for Hammamet's International Festival, the twin of Carthage's. The (late) evening performances are held in the mock-Greek theatre which the State, having bought Sebastian's villa in 1959, built in 1964.

The International Cultural Centre

Nabeul, ceramic-tiled façade of an 'artist potter's' shop

Nabeul. We have not even the name of the Punic town which Agathocles took and which, allied with Carthage, was likewise razed by Scipio. Caesar, after Thapsus, established Colonia Julia Neapolis here, a colony that Augustus made autonomous. The builders of Nabeul's first hotel discovered the site by accident in 1965; its name of Neapolis (since changed to Aquarius) was thus a foregone conclusion and the resultant excavation (now overgrown again) is visible alongside. In 1738 a Scottish clergyman called Shaw found Nabeul already 'a very thriving town . . . much celebrated for its potteries'. Far more than the newer concern for wrought iron and rush-work, perfumes, bricks and tourists, it is pottery that still preoccupies the modern county-town.

Nabeul's Friday Market is an unintended *pièce de résistance*. The township is busiest on this Muslim day of rest, its *Suq el-Juma'* being a North African cross between Petticoat Lane, a village auction and a jumble sale. The first vast compound contains framed and dated pictures, pots and perfumes, cloth, clothes, kitchenware and cosmetic herbs. A small enclave adjacent sells vegetables and fruit. The next compound is piles of seeds and blood-red peppers, open sacks of nuts and grain, rolls of rush-matting and unwashed, unspun wool, coils of rope, donkey saddles and one corner colourful with rugs. In the livestock section, alongside sheep, cattle and goats, are the camels which for many overseas visitors seem to be the principal attraction.

Dar Chaabane el-Fehri, now almost a suburb of Nabeul, is the centre of the sculpted stonework done to a lesser extent in Tunis and Sfax. The stone comes from Jebel Dar Chaabane, seven miles away; the masons are all locals – and proud of it – and designs are invariably geometric or floral. They are drawn on tracing-paper, perforated with a nail and transferred to the cut stone by the mason, like Nabeul's potters, dabbing on a bag of wet charcoal. Hammer and chisel then gouge out the lines in the obviously soft stone.

Nabeul's 'artist potters' (the local clay being too coarse) import finer kaolin from Khroumiria and elsewhere. They use chemical colours from France instead of the old oxidized-metal powders, for designs that range from Ancient Greece through William Morris to Paul Klee. The 'common potters' are found in a fascinating Babylon-clay warren of kilns and shacks in and off the Rue Sidi Barket. They break up the clods, from the nearby Ghar Tefal pits, in a mule-drawn mill; trample them, moistened, in a quite literal mud-bath, and turn them into bricks, tiles, pots and platters.

Dar Chaabane sculptor

Kelibia. Punic and Roman relics have been found beneath the present, probably 6th-century Byzantine citadel. In 310 BC Agathocles occupied the Punic port which the Greeks had named Aspis. Regulus landed here at the start of the First Punic War and, at the end of the Third, the town was destroyed with its ally, Carthage, only to be revived by the Roman empire as Clupea. The 9th-century Aghlabites repaired and garrisoned; between 1535 and 1547 the Arab town was thrice sacked by the Spaniards and thrice rebuilt. Also, partially, by the Turkish pasha Ibrahim Sherif in 1704 and by a local benefactor named Suleiman ben Mustafa in the early 19th century.

Since the late 1970s the seven square towers and connecting crenellations have been impressively repointed, and 'rampart walks' part-completed along the 30-foot-high walls. The interior contains a central basin undergoing excavation and an even larger catchment in the south-west corner. In the west wall a ramp has been unearthed whence steps are being laid bare to the beach. A putative chapel, colonnaded and vaulted, has been restored in the northern corner. Below it are lightless, cruel cells; their rings for the captives' chains have been removed, but underneath have been discovered even more inhuman dungeon-tombs. In the lee of the castle the fishing-port is important, and a Roman excavation area neighbours the National Fisheries School.

Kerkouane is considered to be the best preserved Punic town in Africa. Its lowly ruins stretch along the cliffs and a broad semicircular talus – from the ramparts? – encloses the compact settlement. The main street runs parallel to the cliffs, and low restored walls mark not only houses but individual rooms. Water-channels and sunken baths are still clear in the flooring; floors, and even the built-in baths and benches, are often in farmhouse-kitchen red, with white tesserae and sometimes cobalt-blue glass. Oven relics inside the first talus – red sherds and charred pits – actually indicate kitchens. Also inside the talus, a curious Tanit inlaid in the floor is the traditional depiction of this goddess, the Phoenicians' Astarte.

All this is typical Punic domestic: since the possibly 5th-century BC site was 'discovered' in 1952, the only public edifice exposed is what might have been a temple. The absence of administrative buildings led to the popular notion that Kerkouane was a Punic seaside resort: longer heads suggested that any such holiday camp would hardly have needed the nearby necropolis, which was excavated in 1968-69 and again in the 1980s to reveal ceramics, coins, and tombs inscribed with the incumbent's name and occupation in the 4th century BC. An exemplary museum now documents and complements the unspectacular but well-maintained site.

'Punic domestic' remains at Kerkouane

Kelibia's fishing-port and citadel

Korbous is a small spa that takes its thermal rôle seriously. Families came from Roman Carthage to take the waters here just as Tunisians and foreigners do today. Its popularity then lapsed for centuries until Ahmed Bey built the pavilion that in 1901 became the present Établissement Thermal, and the French engineer Lecore Carpentier began the development of the modern town. Old Korbous with its colonnaded, black-and-white arched hostelries is now confined to the left slope of the single street. The right-hand side is wholly 'medico-modern': the rebuilt Clinique Médicale des Thermes and, since 1982, the sand, green and white blocks of the Hôtel des Sources. Downhill, stairs and a tunnel lead to the ex-Roman *étuves* (sweating-rooms) of Ain Araga. Focal centre is the Ain Chefa bath-house, originally beylical but extended in the 1970s. Beside it, the sunken, tiled and balustraded Ain Sebia (Virgin's Spring) offers free bowls of water like weak spinach juice. Further along the seafront, Ain Atrous is curious: rushing out of a Greek-oracle site in the cliff face, its 50° water streams down the rocks, leaving mineral streaks and an odour of sulphur.

Zaghouan, a governorate since 1978, is fast expanding into a sizeable mountainside county-town, with administrative and ministry buildings. The sorry-looking arch (2nd century AD), only relic of Roman Ziqua, is remarkable solely for its two alcoves, from which Roman statues once looked out over the valley, and for its simplist cow's head on the keystone. From the main Rue Habib Bourguiba the narrow Rue Sidi Ali Azouz climbs past the old Great Mosque and the exquisite, early 19th-century Qubba of Sidi Ali Azuz, and on to the Nymphaeum. The Roman Temple of the Waters, built under Hadrian, retains its walls with their twelve niches for statues, but is defaced by modern graffiti and 'restorations'.

Thuburbo Maius, rich from the cornland around, grew steadily from a settled Berber site to a Phoenician city that sided with Carthage in the final Punic War. Punitively taxed but not demolished by Scipio, the town was chosen in 27 BC for one of Octavius' colonies of veterans. The prosperous Julia Aurelia Commoda of the 2nd century AD waned in the 3rd; revived in the 4th century by Constantine II, the Respublica Felix fell victim to the Vandals and was abandoned in Byzantine times. 'Rediscovered' in 1875, the fine ruins were unearthed and re-erected in 1912.

The capitol is conspicuous from the entrance with its 28-foot columns raised in AD 168. Contiguous is the 160-foot-square forum laid in AD 161-192 and restored in 376. Deep chambers behind the capitol contain oil-presses: as Rome declined, tradesmen and peasants moved in and made workshops of the imperial monuments.

Thuburbo Maius

The Temple of Mercury (AD 211), recognizable by its circular design, occupies the south-west corner of the paved *agora* (market-place) which adjoins the forum. To the south-east lie the imposing Winter Baths, with twenty rooms, a four-column portico and mosaic-floored *frigidarium*, pools circular and square and latrines with a rectangle of urinals.

The Petronii Portico was built in AD 225 by Petronius Felix and Sons. Here was found the Bardo Museum's 'podgy boxers' mosaic, which identified the splendid edifice as a *palaestra* (gymnasium). The adjoining Summer Baths, restored in AD 361, consist of 30,000 square feet of marble and mosaic, and three baths. Directly behind the portico, the small sanctuary was dedicated to Asclepius, patron of sport, and directly above this, through the re-erected arch, the Temple of Baal is a curious example of the Romans' looking back to pagan creeds.

Testour was founded on the site of the Roman Tichilla by Moors (and some Jews) expelled from Spain in 1609. It is, not unnaturally, a self-conscious Andalusian curiosity with its wide alleys, Toledo-church-tower minaret and *teja* roofs. In 1967 the annual June Festival of Maalouf was started, then an all-night, now a week-long eisteddfod of classical Andalusian music. The rambling 17th-century Great Mosque has, unusually, two courtyards, the second with a curious sun-dial and a minaret in classic Spanish (and Christian) style. Off the main street lie the Mosque of Sidi Saghair es-Sai, which the locals call *Jami' en-Nakhla* (Palm Mosque, because of a tree that survived in situ until 1982) and, similarly brick-minareted, the restored 17th-century Mosque of Sidi Abdul-Latif. In the Rue du 26 février 1953 stand the Mosque of Sidi Nasser el-Qarawashi and, at the top, his green-tiled zawia (1733).

Testour, the Great Mosque

Dougga dominates Tunisian archaeology – for its site, entirety and extent. Bulla Regia half hides underground, Thuburbo Maius lies low in its valley, but at 2000 feet Dougga's 62 acres of monuments are equal to the pre-eminence. Its theatres, temples, thermae and capitol overlook the deep Oued Khalled and exploit the panorama.

In Dougga's case the Berber connections are not the usual conjecture but of great significance. The Libyco-Punic Mausoleum was raised, probably in the 2nd century BC, by architect Abarish for the Numidian prince Ateban: its dedicatory plaque, inscribed synonymously in the Berber and Punic tongues, was of Rosetta-stone value to linguists.

Massinissa having allied with Rome against Carthage, the 'Libyco-Punic' Thugga was not seized or razed in 146 BC. But his offspring having supported the Pompeians, the city became part of Caesar's Africa Nova after Thapsus. Dougga thereafter gradually grew into the Municipium Thuggense created by Septimius in AD 205. Though never numbering more than 5000 inhabitants, its size and prosperity throughout the following century are attested by the present-day site. Declining with the Roman empire, surviving the Vandals, revived by the Byzantines and never since wholly abandoned, Dougga's historical continuity is such that some writers consider the peasants of Nouvelle Dougga to be pure 'Thuggenses' still.

The capitol, one of the finest remains of Roman North Africa, was constructed in AD 167 in honour of Jupiter, Juno and Minerva. It is reached from the theatre by a Roman shopping street, its paving pierced by central drains, scored on the inclines to hold the horses' hooves and rutted with the passage of countless chariot wheels. The street opens into the Square of the Winds, laid between AD 180 and 192 and named from the 25-foot-wide 'compass' of winds inscribed in the paving in the 3rd century. Southwards, below the mosque, a paved alley crosses the market and a lower area of mosaics, columns and house-walls, and 22 steps descend into the colonnaded 'changing rooms' and the magnificent halls of the 3rd-century Winter Baths.

The theatre, erected in AD 166-169, had a reputed capacity of 3500. Earthenware pots imbedded in the topmost walls ensured perfect acoustics; the *proscenium* (stage) drops to the orchestra in the usual alternate semicircular and rectangular alcoves; when it rains the orchestra becomes the catchment area, with pipes draining off under the stage; holes and slots in the stage floor were for the scenery 'props', and a frieze in foot-high letters, now fallen and broken, topped the backcloth-colonnade.

Dougga, the Temple of Saturn

The Temple of Saturn stands unforgettable on the skyline. Behind the landmark of its three whole and three half columns, the temple (AD 195) has subterranean vaults, a central *area* pell-mell with masonry and an odd, half-inch imprint of feet in the paving. Towards the theatre, above the road, is the 5th-century church with steps down to three dwarf and two larger coffins, one of which is inscribed 'Victoria'; the half-cupola of the sanctuary of Neptune and the Christian Basilica's sunken courtyard of sarcophagi.

The capitol's monumental stairs rise from the *area ante capitolium*, whence humbler steps descend to the forum. Round this, and disfiguring the capitol also, stand the Byzantine walls of reused Roman stone. North of the capitol is an interesting area of antique litter and, conspicuous to the west, the Arch of Severus Alexander (AD 222-235) or Bab er-Rumia (Christian Girl's Gate). The track beyond leads through olive-groves to the contemporary Temple of Caelestis, constructed under Severus Alexander (and reconstructed by Monsieur Poinssot).

Dougga, the Arch of Severus Alexander

Makthar was founded, a protectorate hill-station, by Captain Bordier in 1887, and he it was who first excavated the Roman Mactaris. A tophet and temples to Baal Hammon and Hathor Miskar testify to a 1st-century BC town, built by the Phoenicians on Berber terrain and recorded, in the semitically vowel-less Punic script, as 'Mktrm'. This linguistic affinity of ancient and modern seems to apply topographically too: today's scarcely prosperous township covers one slope of the steep Oued Saboun, the opulent ancient site the other. A Punic tophet and a Roman portal lie in between – called, in hybrid language, the Arch of Bab el-Ain.

In the museum, the relics collected by Gilbert-Charles Picard from 1944 to 1959 illustrate Makthar's past: Punic and neo-Punic stelae from as late as the 2nd century AD (because Makthar, remote, sheltered the descendants of Carthage's refugees and was incorporated late into Africa Nova; inscriptions, mosaics and emperors' heads from the 2nd-century heyday (crowned by Marcus Aurelius' creation of a colonia in AD 180) and Christian tombs and epitaphs from the 3rd-4th centuries.

The colonnaded schola housed the Juventutes, a youth organization used in war as auxiliaries and in peace as policemen and postmen. Their inscription to Domitian, from AD 88, can be seen in the museum. Their 1st-century premises were rebuilt in the 2nd century, made a church in the 4th, 'vandalized' then restored by the Byzantines. The remarkable building adjoining is a clover-leaf of apses added in the 4th century to a 2nd-century original; in the rectangular stone *auges* the Juventutes measured the peasants' taxes in kind.

The baths are the finest of all Tunisia's
thermae. Completed by AD 200, they
still convey much of their pristine splendour with walls and vaults conscientious-
ly restored, fine polychrome flooring
and that in the *frigidarium* a black-
and-white mosaic maze. The baths are
situated below the 5th-century Basilica of Hildeguns and the hilltop
forum, unmistakable with its arch
of triumph dedicated, as the frieze
says, to the emperor Trajan in
AD 116.

Le Kef, the Mosque of Sidi Bou
Makhlouf in the 1970s: the interior of
the cupola was a masterpiece of
sculpted, painted stucco until crudely
plastered white.

The 14th-century Mosque of Sidi Bou Makhlouf forms an attractive complex with the old Great Mosque and the renovated basilica which, besieged by statuary, capitals and plinths, has become a lapidary museum. Above, the kasba crowns Le Kef. It was built by Mohammed Bey in 1679, its ramparts added by Ali Bey in the 1740s. Back along the Rue Ali ben Trad, the Regional Museum of Popular Arts and Traditions was opened in 1979. Exhibits illustrate local crafts and life-styles; feminine adornment is detailed right down to separate displays 'for the Waist', 'for the Breast', 'for the Ears' etc., while a life-size replica of a nomad encampment has even the appropriate odour. There are farm-tools, pottery and, since 1983, Hebrew epitaphs, papyrus Thora and silver plaques from the relinquished synagogue.

Le Kef (The Rock) is unofficially 'capital' of the border region. In this Carthaginian dependency, first recorded in 256 BC, the mercenary army assembled and mutinied after the First Punic War. The colony of Sicca Veneria which Octavian established took its name from a temple to Venus/Astarte in which the 'Punic matrons' practised sacred prostitution. Paradoxically, the 2nd-3rd-century colonia became an important Christian centre, and monasteries, as in Europe, meant material prosperity here too. The Arab invasion put an end to both; only with the Turkish regency was Le Kef reanimated as a beylical bulwark against the pashas of Algiers.

The Mosque of Sidi Bou Makhlouf, Le Kef

Sousse is a compromise between Tunis and Hammamet, a city in its own right like the one, a popular resort like the other. If the beaches, although excellent, are not as exquisite as Hammamet's and the Sahel hinterland of sebkha and olive-groves less exotic, Sousse's medina, museum and catacombs, its esplanade, cinemas and pavement cafés, its prestigious adjunct of Kantaoui/Sousse-Nord, all give it the variety that Hammamet lacks.

The city's past is correspondingly varied. Before Carthage but after Utica, the Phoenicians established here a port of unknown name, and near this flourishing town (a large tophet has been found) Hannibal disembarked at the end of his campaign in Italy. For repudiating Carthage in the Third Punic War, Sousse was made a free city by Scipio, an honour which it thereafter lost for supporting Pompey's

allies against Caesar. From the colony of Hadrumetum established by the emperor Trajan, little remains except mosaics in the Bardo and the Kasba museums. The now-Christian town was renamed Hunericopolis by the Vandals, and Justinianopolis by the Byzantines. The Arabs reduced it to Susa and temporary oblivion. Having embarked here for their conquest of Sicily, the Aghlabites then built extensively – ribat, kasba and Great Mosque – even though Sousse remained Kairouan's rival. That of Tunis, too, during the beylical civil war of the 1730s. The town was attacked by Ali Pasha's gunboats, as it had been by the 12th-century Normans and the 16th-century Spaniards. And was to be yet again by the Genoese, the French and finally the Allies. Their heavy attacks in 1943 led to the re-building of the modern town.

Sousse Medina is best entered via the Place des Martyrs, the breach of the old Sea Gate made in the walls by the bombing of 1943. Prominent opposite is the ribat, most important of the monastery-fortresses with which the Aghlabites picketed the coast from Ceuta to Alexandria to forestall Christian attacks. Sousse Ribat was completed in AD 821 (at a cost of 18,000 dinars). The barbican gate has four apertures above for the portcullis and/or boiling oil; there follows a plain and reworked courtyard, a first gallery of cells (their antique contents now removed to Kairouan) and, beneath the Kufic inscription above its entrance, 73 steps up the *Nador* (watch-tower). Used for spotting enemy aircraft in the War, it offers the best view of the new town and the old.

The Great Mosque, behind the Bab el-Bahar, is distinguished by its kiosk-minarets. A courtyard of galleries, the southernmost added in 1675 and all renovated in 1975, then the prayer-room, impressive in its simplicity, not in its decoration. The vaulted naves of perfect arches stretch away like a study in infinity. Roman capitals are imbedded in or lean against the massive cruciform bases. Built in 851, the prayer-room was extended in the 10th, 11th and 17th centuries and restored in 1964-65.

Sousse-Nord had added a new dimension to Tunisia's tourism. In the mid-1970s the authorities created, on an attractive but virgin stretch of coast, a self-contained holiday centre complete with a yacht basin and tournament golf course. Around the ten-acre, 340-berth marina the 'first Mediterranean garden port' was inaugurated in 1979: arched, cobbled alleys, gardened squares and lamplit quays already give the place an 'old world' charm.

Kairouan. The Muslim conquerors, on their third incursion in 668 AD, chose this site for their capital. It lay on important caravan routes; it was equidistant from their coastal enemies, the Byzantines, and those in the hills, the Berbers, and, as the leader Oqba ibn Nafi arrived, there opened at his feet a spring in which he found a gold cup lost years before in Mecca. This clinched the spot's sanctity. Raising Kairouan to the status of national capital in the 9th century, the Aghlabites developed a reportedly sumptuous city, which the Beni Hilal laid low in 1057.

Today the people of Kairouan number some 532,700. They manufacture carpets and leather- and brassware, and have restored walls and mosques to make a picturesque city, which they deck with flags and fairy-lights for the festival of Mouled, the Prophet Mohammed's birthday (a moveable feast as arbitrary as Christmas and ignored by strict Muslims elsewhere).

The Aghlabite Pools adjoin the suburb of shrines that are appropriately one's first sight of this holy city when arriving from Tunis or Sousse. Constructed in the 9th century, one large and one small pool were restored in 1969 to their (putatively) pristine state; two others have been excavated to the east and several more are suspected round about.

The ramparts, refaced and repointed, belie their 900 years (although the 1052 structure was repaired in 1712 – and breached again when the Axis troops needed rock for their landing-strip). From the Aghlabite Pools and the Barber's Mosque, the triple gateway of the Porte de Tunis opens on to the medina.

The original Great Mosque of Oqba ibn Nafi was rebuilt in 695, extended in 743, replaced in 774 and again, finally, in 836, when Ziyadat-Allah raised the whole plot some ten feet. His Aghlabite structure was renovated thoroughly in 1025, 1294, 1618 and 1970-72 (for the town's 1300th anniversary). It is not only one of the most historically hybrid mosques in Africa, it is also the oldest and most revered. Tunisians are said to believe that the religious duty of a pilgrimage to Mecca can be redeemed by visiting Kairouan seven times.

Ramparts of the medina of Kairouan

The midha (ablutions room) faces the mosque's west wall and marks the entrance to the colonnaded courtyard. In the paving, seven wells have rims furrowed by generations of bucket-ropes; another is patterned in horseshoe cavities – to decant the rainwater. To the southeast stands the magnificent façade of the prayer-room. Its 'forest of columns' is perhaps a cliché but no other description is adequate: columns from Roman Carthage and Sousse; some Byzantine, some Aghlabite; columns inscribed with Christian crosses; columns you must squeeze between if you are not to be judged too fat for Paradise; columns in marble, three even in porphyry (given, they say, by Charlemagne in return for Saint Cyprian's remains). Their capitals are Roman, Byzantine or Arab. Since 1970 some are Tunisian too.

The minaret was completed in 836: 114 feet high and with Christian fish sculpted in some of its 128 steps. It should align with Sidi Oqba's original mihrab, but does not because the Umayyad caliph Hisham used for its base an existing cistern. It is not widely known that the Great Mosque, an Islamic sanctum, occupies a Christian site. Its ground-plan was dictated by a line of Byzantine villas (which the Arab geographer Al-Bakri mentioned, Nu'man ibn Sa'ad destroyed and Oqba himself cleared of snakes). Excavating, and confirming this in 1968, an Italian team made amends with its findings that the Great Mosque's was at least the oldest minaret-base known.

The Zawia of Sidi Sahib is a delightful assemblage of patios, corridors and 'cells' for the medersa pupils. Its main cupola was completed in 1629, the minaret in 1690. In the final patio, resplendent with ceramic-tiled and sculpted-plaster walls, Sidi Sahib's tomb is draped in white and green, adorned with prints of Mecca and usually screened by a cluster of sifsaris. Its 7th-century incumbent (really Abu Jama' el-Balawi) was called Sidi Sahib (the Companion) because of his association with the Prophet Mohammed. The zawia itself is called the 'Barber's Mosque' because Abu Jama' possessed three hairs of the Prophet's beard.

Sbeitla, mentioned only in later lists of bishoprics, is documented by its monuments and inscriptions alone. Of the latter, the earliest dates from Vespasian (AD 69-79). The prosperity of Sufetula under the Roman empire is attested by Diocletian's arch of triumph (c. AD 290); by olive-presses, three vestigial thermae and the theatre, prettily sited beside the oued with its orchestra paving and some seats remaining; by the unexcavated but distinctively shaped amphitheatre (nearest the hotel) and above all by the forum's famous temples. The monumental Arch of Antoninus Pius gives on to the forum, with Christian masons' marks in its part-intact paving and shopping-booths visible on the south side. On the west, the three temples rise resplendent: in the absence of inscriptions we can only assume that, as at Dougga, they were dedicated in the 2nd century AD to Jupiter, Juno and Minerva.

Byzantine walling encumbers them and, opposite the museum at the entrance, three fortresses are further relics of this 6-7th-century seat of the patrician-bishops and Tunisia's ephemeral capital. But Sufetula's distinction is its churches from the 4th and 5th centuries. North of the three temples, the Church of Vitalis is identified by the beautiful white 'upholstery' of its baptismal font, and by the saint's name in crude mosaic. The nearby Church of Bellator has a similarly curvaceous baptistery, the body of the kirk being a square colonnade. The Vandals conducted worship here too: they converted the Church of Servus (near the theatre) from a pagan temple into a Donatist chapel and, between the churches of Vitalis and Bellator, a house was adapted as the tomb of St Jucundus, a Catholic martyred by the fellow-Christian Vandals.

Kasserine is, thanks to its cellulose factory, an active county-town. Its name 'Two Towers' derives from the two roadside Roman mausoleums. (Inscribed on the second are 110 lines of poetry to one Flavius Secundus.) Further vestiges of Cillium, the 1st-century AD municipium and 3rd-century colonia to which St Augustin contributed a 5th-century monastery, crown the hill: an inscribed arch of triumph (3rd century), a vaulted church and (over the hill, beside the oued) a theatre like Dougga's but smaller, with balustrades in place and twenty broken rows of seats.

Sbeitla: temples, forum and arch of Antoninus Pius (left)
Kasserine, Roman mausoleum (above)

Monastir. In 1830 Grenville Temple wrote: 'The face of the town, its battlements and towers . . . is very pretty'. Still it appears as an opera backcloth of battlements, minarets, marabouts, towers and cupolas: a town-planner's model larger than life. The settlement's start in life as Punic Rous Penna; Caesar's garrison of Ruspina; the town's 11th-century (but temporary) replacement of Kairouan as Tunisia's religious capital; its key defensive position throughout the Middle Ages; the Muslim soldiers' belief that three days' garrison duty in this first ribat-town

vouchsafed them Paradise . . . all are of less importance in Tunisian eyes than the fact that Habib Bourguiba was born here on 3 August 1903 – or was it 1901?

The veneration is all-pervading: as one rounds the corniche, the Bourguiba family mausoleum is the immediate, unmistakable focal centre. The resplendent shrine of buff stone, blue ceramics and Carrara marble was rebuilt even bigger in 1978. In 1980 came the twin minarets, grey-marble and gold-tipped; then the four gadrooned domes, one dazzling golden, three

gilded green behind (in honour of the former president's father, mother and first wife).

The Martyrs' Memorial is one of the two open-polygonal kiosks that decorate the main square. Amidst the tombs behind, the Qubba of Sidi Ali el-Mezeri (a 12th-century imam) has the reputation of curing ailing babies and being imbued afresh each Friday morning with a divine aroma. Near the shrine stood until 1980 a Cemetery Gate inscribed with lines by the Imam Mezeri in honour of a Princess Mona (whence, according to the locals, the name 'Monastir'. Experts have nothing better to offer). The portal – like many of the well-aligned graves, all simple, most white – has been sacrificed to the lengthy sward that precedes the ex-president's tomb.

The Ribat of Harthema was built in 796 by Harthema ibn Ayun, a general with Harun ar-Rashid. It has been rebuilt or reworked four times (9th, 11th, 17th and 19th centuries) and now requires expert study to say precisely what came when. Suffice it to say that from the northern ramparts of the Men's Ribat, above the entrance, there is a fine view of the cemetery, and from the *Nador* (watch-tower), with its 87 steps, an even better panorama of the town. The former mosque between the Men's Ribat and the Women's (to the south) was in 1958 installed as a small islamic museum. This contains wood from the Kairouan Great Mosque's minbar, Aghlabite bookbindings and Umayyad sculpted bones; inscribed papyrus and illuminated pages; Fatimite combs, and gold and silver coins; Abbassid and Fatimite earthenware; Sanhaji glass, Coptic tissues and Persian miniatures. A gate, restored in 1970 but subsequently closed, led from the Women's Ribat to the adjacent Great Mosque (9th-century, reworked in the 10th, with a simple façade and stern, vaulted interior).

The Habib Bourguiba Mosque was constructed, behind the demolished Bab Derb, in 1963-66. Recently the showpiece has been not only locked to non-Muslims, its windows have also been blocked. Of the marble fountains and paving in the courtyard, the nineteen teak doors sculpted in Kairouan, the 86 gleaming columns and magnificent chandeliers in the prayer-room . . . not even a glimpse is possible.

Prayer-room of the Habib Bourguiba Mosque

93

remnant of the 35-foot wall by which the hated Mahdi shut off his isthmus capital. The Friday-morning market is unique: village women hawking their gilt and sequinned *gilets de mariage*, while peddlars squat weighing out gold and silver. The old Dar el-Himma, once the Sfar Mosque, became in 1977 a Traditional Silk-weaving Museum, with model looms and notices explaining how the art was brought by Libyan Jews to Mahdia in the 19th century, recognized as a craft guild in 1956 and protected by import barriers against cheap competition from Lyons.

The Great Mosque is a masterpiece of its kind, well proportioned, dignified and unadorned. It was founded, without minaret, by caliph Ubaid-Allah in 921. In the courtyard the Zirites massacred his Shi'ite co-religionists in 1016, thereby incurring the Fatimite caliph's wrath, and prompting the Hilalian invasion. The same courtyard was made a Spanish cemetery by Charles V, who used the mosque as a stop-gap church, and blew it up when he departed in 1554. Sporadically patched up thereafter, the edifice had collapsed completely by the 1950s. The consequent total reconstruction (1961-65) is in perfect imitation Fatimite. The monumental portal, reserved originally for the Mahdi's entourage (and the first of its kind in Islamic architecture), gives on to the courtyard, and the seven massive doors with their gargantuan black studs, on to the prayer-room.

The Borj er-Ras (Headland Tower) overlooks the cliff-top cemetery that stretches to the tip of Cape Africa. Worked in its facade is a cross-bow and a caricature tiger, and above the inner door an inscribed plaque which, translated, reads: 'This blessed Fort was Completed with the Help of God – may His Name be Praised – by the Endeavours of His servant Abu Abdallah Mohammed Pasha – may God give him Triumph – on 6.9.1595'. The strategically winding entrance of this former French prison contains antiquarian photographs and capitals; the hall was in 1984 almost a museum; the courtyard is the setting for the annual Nuits de Mahdia (July and August *son et lumière*) and the crenellated walls are panoramic. The road below runs on along a shore of ramparts (which Charles V demolished along with the mosque) and past the single arch of the old Sea Gate, which opened on to the Fatimite port.

Mahdia lies on a promontory site that is unique: both Phoenicians and Romans appreciated it as a naval base; the Fatimites exploited it as an easily defended capital; the Arab historian Ibn Khaldun praised it as a 'dagger held in the fist', while his French contemporary Froissart went one better by calling the isthmus 'Africa' *tout court*. The name survives in this 'Cape Africa'. The site saved the Mahdi in 944-945 from an eight-month siege by the Kharijite horde of Abu Yazid (whom he crucified on the Skifa el-Kahla then stuffed with straw). The Zirites fled here in 1057 as the Beni Hilal neared Kairouan; Roger II's Norman forces evicted them in 1148, only to be ousted in their turn by the Almohads twelve years later. In 1390 a Franco-Genoese fleet failed to take the port, which was occupied by Dragut in 1549 and, after triple bombardment, by Charles V from 1550 to 1554. The deys and beys brought new blood, several local families descending from the Turks' janissaries and other Balkan subjects. Under the French protectorate Mahdia grew into Tunisia's foremost fishing-port and, with the Sahel's olive-oil and the salt worked locally until 1938, its largest canning centre.

The fishing-port's long orderly quay becomes a lively market every Friday morning: clothes, fruit, vegetables and local essentials such as camel saddles. Equally colourful then too, the Bab Zouila belies its alias of Skifa el-Kahla (Sombre Gate). Rebuilt in 1554, it is the only

Mahdia's fishing-port

'Cape Africa', the headland cemetery

El-Jem, the world's sixth largest Roman amphitheatre, is easy to visualize whole. The three tiers of arcades could seat some 30,000 spectators; the games here became famous and drew crowds from much of Roman Africa. They would file in by the vaulted galleries and the steep stairs around; the emperor would take his place at whichever end was in the shade and, from the dungeons below (which were found only in 1904), the gladiators and Christian martyrs, incarcerated for days beside the lions, would be brought out to fight or die.

El-Jem acquired the inevitable legends: a tunnel to Mahdia (still unearthed) was large enough for elephants to drag up the imported rock for building, but too narrow for them to turn back: another led to the catacombs of Sousse. The arena was 'proof against scorpions', so the locals protected their homes with its stone.

The Romans built this 'colosseum' in AD 230 – 484 feet long, 403 wide, 117 high – to persuade the resurgent Berbers that Rome was not declining. (Gordian was 80 and senile when the local landlords, overtaxed by Rome,

proclaimed him emperor here in AD 238. He reigned for a few weeks before being defeated by the emperor Maximinus, losing his son and killing himself at Carthage.) The amphitheatre was probably not the scene of the legendary last stand of the Berber Boadicea, El-Kahena, as many believe, and the walls were first breached by Mohammed Bey to evict rebels hiding here in 1695. Between 1974 and 1980 the amphitheatre was impressively restored, thanks in large part to the Gulbenkian Foundation.

As further proof of Roman Thysdrus' prosperity in the 2nd and 3rd centuries – from the 37,000 acres of olive-groves that the emperor Hadrian promoted and El-Kahena later burned in a scorched earth policy – there is the site of Bir ez-Zit and, on the hilltop opposite the museum, a second amphitheatre seating 10,000.

El-Jem, the Roman amphitheatre

Sfax. Ronald Firbank once described Sfax as the most beautiful city in the world. Even the mayor laughed when I told him. The city, Tunisia's second largest, is a Mediterranean Coventry: part industrial, part historic; heavily bombed in the War – its fine Hôtel de Ville remaining as the blocks around went down – and thereafter widely rebuilt. Their compatriots look on the Sfaxis as slightly untypical: thrifty, hard-working, shrewd (*Baccalauréat* passes here are the country's best) and somehow more Nordic than Mediterranean.

This may explain their constant prosperity since Roman times. Most vestiges of the Roman Taparura are in the Hôtel de Ville Museum. Better preserved, and Sfax's main claim to 'beauty', are the 9th-century walls of the Aghlabite medina. Thanks perhaps to its long-established wealth from olives, cereals, cloth, fruit, fish and perfume, the 'Capital of the South' alone survived as an independent state after the Hilalian invasion. True to that tradition, it backed Ali ben Ghedahem's revolt against the bey in 1864 and succumbed to the French in 1881 only after naval bombardment. Its commercial significance increased when Sfax became the railhead for the line to Metlaoui's phosphate mines. Deposits of oil discovered both on shore and off have since the mid-1970s given the city's fortunes a further fillip.

Sfax, the Dar Jellouli Museum

Sfax Museum, painting on glass

Sfax Medina. To the left of the three
apertures added in 1944, the original
passage-way of the Bab ed-Divan (the
Council Gate; 1306) makes a worthy
start to a medina almost as charming as
Tunis'. (Reputedly accessible to Christians only since 1832, it is now cluttered
with notices and signs to aid the infidels.) Behind the food and handicraft
shops in the gateway stands the *Jami'
el-Azuzein* (the Mosque of the Two
Old Women) and uphill that of Sidi
El-Bahri (the 'Sea Lord'). The Museum
of Popular Arts and Traditions was installed in 1966 in the Dar Jellouli (early
18th century, renovated 1728). The
galleries of this Andalusian palace are
quite as well worth seeing as its collection of costumes, arms and cosmetics,
interiors, furniture and household
implements. Upstairs exhibits are
'Costumes féminins de Sfax' (but no
longer circumcision costumes and
customs). Beside displays of Arab
calligraphic styles are some of the
finest examples to be found of
Tunisian painting on glass.

Sfax medina, metalware

Kerkenna. A 'Society for the Exploitation of the Islands of Kerkenna' was founded in 1961 to ensure a revival of the local economy: now the islanders are pinning their hopes on Sfax's new international airport. The Greeks as early as the 5th century BC knew the islands as Kyrannis (where Hannibal sought refuge in 195 BC). Caesar sent troops to the Roman Cercina to seize the Pompeians' supplies, and in AD 15 one Caius Sempronius Gracchus was exiled to Kerkenna and executed – for seducing the emperor's daughter. Both subsequent invasion (by Byzantines, Arabs and Normans) and lack of water and work (just sponges, dates, alfa and olives, a few vines, figs, sheep and fish) explain the mass migration to the mainland, where the menfolk are mostly employed as waiters and restaurateurs.

This idyllic backwater lies an hour or so by ferry from the hectic city of Sfax. Around Sidi Yousef, where the ferry docks, the arrow-shapes and zigzags of palm-fronds in the shallows are fish-traps. Amongst them nestle the hollowed blocks in which, hopefully, the octopuses hide; the Kerkennis catch them, by hand, for freezing in Sfax and export to Japan.

Jerba. If Jerba is usually tagged on to the end of books about Tunisia, it is not only because the island lies like a geographical afterthought down by the Libyan border. Idyllic but detached, Jerba is also an outsider in politics, religion and population.

Our knowledge of Jerba begins in myth. Ulysses, sailing from Troy, reached a desert island where the people lived blissfully on lotus. Jerba, Majorca and Minorca all claim to identify with 'Lotus-land' so Jerba, for extra legend-cover, also believes itself to be Ogygia, where Calypso held Ulysses captive. History starts with the Romans, who built Girba, Haribus, Meninx and Tipasa, perhaps on Phoenician foundations. Jerba's contribution to the classical era is appropriately small-scale: the emperors Gallus and Valerian were born here – to reign a joint total of nine years (AD 251-260). Vandals, Byzantines and Hilalians found little to destroy, but the island's useful anchorage on a flat, sandy coast attracted the mediaeval sea powers. Roger II, that piecemeal empire-builder who ruled Sicily, Prussia and Jerusalem, took it in 1134. Its conquerors thereafter read like a list of prize-winners: Roger de Loria 1284, Raymond Montaner 1331, the Moroccan Merinites 1335, Pedro Navarro 1510, Charles V 1535. The sieges and slaughters reached a climax in 1560 when the Pope's French, Spanish and Neapolitan troops joined forces with the Knights of Malta to crush once and for all the pirate lair that Dragut had made of Jerba . . . but only 5-6000 Christians survived the first encounter in May and fled to the Borj el-Kebir. On 31 July Dragut evicted and massacred them, piling their skulls on the beach. There was some resistance to the French army in 1881 but the two World Wars passed Jerba by.

The Jerbans throughout all this continued to grow olives and palms, weave carpets, and fish. They were also inbreeding to a distinctive type: short, long-headed and sallow-skinned. This perhaps lies behind their present feeling of detachment. In religion, too, there is isolation. The Jerbans welcomed the Muslim invaders in the 7th century then turned to an unorthodox sect of Islam: as Kharijites still, they are Muslim Quakers, slightly austere, egalitarian and mild-mannered, believing in conscience as a rule of conduct. Nature more than religion

however has dictated their recent history. Lack of water had always limited progress and, in the last two centuries, led to mass emigration.

The island measures eighteen by seventeen and a half miles at its longest and widest; the generally blissful beaches extend for almost 80 miles and the highest point above sea-level is all of 182 feet. Exports are primarily carpets but also fish, sponges, pottery and soap. The *fsaqia* seen in every village is the classical *impluvium*, an area of sloping concrete designed to catch and channel precious rainwater. Of the 213 mosques all are different and most unique, minor wonders so coated and recoated with white-wash and plaster that they seem to have melted and set again off centre.

Houmt Souk is the island's only urban centre and ipso facto its capital. The road from the hotels approaches past the Zawia of Sidi Isma'il and, pretty on its promontory, the Sidi Zaid Mosque (or zawia: praying in both, Jerbans make no distinction). Beyond the beach where the women wash wool, the road forks through town and grows into the main square from which the name Houmt Souk (Market Quarter) derives.

The Borj el-Kebir (Great Tower) stands prominent on the sea-shore. A Roman statue found in recent excavations indicates the site's first occupants. Roger de Loria, given Jerba in 1284 as the King of Aragon's reward for taking it, built a first fort. This the Hafsite sultan Abu Faris razed when, in the early 15th century, he built the present edifice to help the islanders withstand Spanish attacks. Seizing the citadel in 1560, Dragut had restored it by 1567. (The local name Borj Ghazi Mustafa stems from his clerk of works) (who is the namesake, but not the incumbent, of the tomb on top.) Since 1971 the pile has been excavated deep and impressively restored. Further along the beach, a simple pyramid commemorates the Tower of Skulls. Dragut's macabre anti-Christian trophy stood here from 1560 until 1848, when the European colony prevailed upon the bey to have it removed to the Christian cemetery.

The Regional Museum, installed in 1968-69 in the Zawia of Sidi Zituni, has exhibits well displayed and labelled, albeit in French and sometimes only in Arabic, of local costumes, jewellery (in an exquisite 'honeycomb' cupola), household implements and pottery (including the 66-gallon *duh*), a mock-potters' workshop in the former cistern below, and coffers carved, painted and studded abundantly for clothes and/or coffins.

Hara Kebira (Big Ghetto), Hara Seghira (Little Ghetto): the names are self explanatory. How and when the Hebrew community came to Jerba is not known. The Jews themselves date their presence here from the Babylonian Captivity in 590 BC; historians opt for Titus' destruction of the Temple in AD 70; the only evidence is the 10th-century tomb of one Cohen. Certain is the Jerban Jews' racial purity, proved by their features, and their decline. Of the 5000 resident in 1956, some 750 and 290 now remain in Hara Kebira and Hara Seghira

Jewellery worked in Hara Kebira

The Ghriba, reading rabbi

respectively. The reason is the pull of Israel, not any local anti-semitism. Hara Kebira boasts a large Hebrew cemetery, the styleless Dkhtia Synagogue and silversmiths who still work gold and silver in ancient Byzantine designs.

The Ghriba is a synagogue famed throughout the Middle East and centre of an international pilgrimage each Passover. Even writers insisting on the Israelites' arrival in AD 70 accept that the Ghriba was founded '600 years before Christ'. A holy stone fell from heaven to mark the site and a mysterious foreign girl (a *ghriba*) appeared, helped the builders with miracles and gave the place its name. The present building may date from 1920. Beyond the arch is the Pilgrims' Hostel and, opposite, the wooden doors to an interior unique rather than inspirational.

Ajim is Jerba's principal port, where fishermen harpoon their four-foot bass and groupers, fetch sponges from ten fathoms and surface with reports of a village submerged in the bay (which may or may not be the ancient Lake of Triton).

Guellala lies scattered over hills of palms and well-heads, its kilns smoking ceaselessly beside the high piled pots. These are the standard coarse gargoulettes but the shops, now business-like to left and right, have other delightful shapes as well as cheap and ingenious 'terra-cotta tricks': pots with rims irregularly 'crenellated' so that fitting the lid is a puzzle, and jugs which are filled from the top, then the bottom, without a drop leaking either way.

Preparing sponges for market, Ajim

Guellala, pots and potteries

Zarzis, really 'Jarjis', is a French-protectorate creation on the site of Roman Gergis. It is the (Friday morning) market-town of a region that was until the 1950s thought to be barren nomads' land. The French experiment in rehabilitating the Accara Beduin to settle and tend olive-groves on soil considered uncultivable succeeded against all expectation. The area's other established asset is its long shore of villas and hotels. Inland, the town relaxes round its cross-roads. It does not have a Turkish fort: this was obliterated in 1978 to make way for the Great Mosque. The latter's minaret looms over the centre, which banks and administrative blocks, a 'Grand Magasin' and small museum all help update.

Ghorfa-shops at Medenine

Ghorfa-hotel, Ksar Haddada

Medenine, where the Eighth army paused before storming the Mareth Line in 1943, and which British Government papers described as a village in 1945, became the county-town of the largest Tunisian governorate – and is still little more than a village. A wide oued divides it ('Medenine' meaning Two Towns). The southern slope is unremarkable with its administrative buildings; quainter are the roads that rise in a trident up the opposite slope, but of greatest interest, along the lower road to Jorf, is the square ksar of ghorfas.

These rock and mud vaults are built one against the other, one above the other, in long terraces up to six storeys high (although Medenine's have collapsed to three). Interiors are approximately 30 feet long, ten wide and six high. Stone steps climb outside, or inside through holes in the ceiling, to upper storeys. Designed as safe storage for the nomads' produce, some ghorfas were on occasions inhabited (despite what government guides and officials maintain: the Arabic word after all means 'room'). At Ksar Haddada and (until recently) Ksar Ouled Debab the ghorfas are not only inhabited but hotels.

Medenine, the main ksar

Douiret, Chenini and Guermessa are well preserved Berber fastnesses. One can only wonder at the fear or zenophobia that drove men to make these crags their homes – so high that there is no longer grazing for their flocks, so steep that sometimes two people cannot pass on the narrow ledge 'streets'. While their forefathers lived here safe from Romans and Arabs, the villagers today are losing out to nature. The Berbers' drift to the towns is a subject of academic study. Just as Frankfurt Jews are bankers and Bradford Jews in cloth, the Berbers of Chenini are the news-vendors of Tunis, those of Douiret its tobacconists and those of Guermessa the porters of the fruit market.

The old town of Douiret clings to a steep squat pinnacle. Ruined ghorfas crown this 'natural edifice'; the mosque dominates the dwellings halfway down, and the lower slopes of grey-green scree end in a cemetery prickly with crude headstones. Chenini Tataouine is included in most 'circuits' of the Ksars and the road from Foum Tataouine is consequently busier. Near to Guermessa, the cliffs close in; the whole face of the natural amphitheatre is holed with ghorfas like a thousand watching eyes.

Old Douiret

The Petite Jara is a lively, colonnaded market-place of clothes and seeds, spices and dried fish, jewellers' and rush-weavers' suqs. Beyond the oued behind, the 11th-century Mosque of Sidi Idris is squat and antiquated with its Roman and Arab capitals.

Gabes the town is a tolerable place, but Gabes the oasis is unforgettable. It may seem odd to travel from Europe to Africa, then drive miles to walk through a market-garden. But Gabes' gardens are unlike any other: four square miles beside the sea, more than 300,000 palms, and from the Ras el-Oued (the Head of the Valley) they can be overlooked entirely. The word is usefully ambiguous, for the oasis starts deep in the canyonlike Oued Gabes. Seen from above, the valley floor is delightful with palms, fruit-trees and rushes mirrored in the waters. A step or two backwards, and the oasis disappears, the desert plateau stretching away apparently unbroken.

The town's history is not fully known. Perhaps a Punic trading station preceded the Roman colony of Tacapae; perhaps Berbers and Byzantines settled here before Sidi Boulbaba, the Prophet's barber, built the first mosque in the 680s. What

Arabs, Spanish and Turks may have left behind vanished, like much of the French-protectorate town, first in the bombardments of 1943 then in the floods of 1962.

The Shrine of Sidi Boulbaba occupies a hilltop out of town on the road to Matmata. The original mosque/medersa, built in 1692, was in 1969 restored for the Museum of Popular Arts and Traditions which finally opened in 1984. Although its minaret (planned as 130 feet) stopped short at 102, the new mosque is more prominent (1974-77). More venerated is Sidi Boulbaba's mausoleum: heavy with incense and stock-piled with carpets; hung with Qoranic texts and pictures of Mecca; precious with silver incense-holders; decorative with Roman or Siamese-twinned pillars, and fronted since 1974 by a court-yard which Christians may tread.

Inside the Shrine of Sidi Boulbaba, Gabes

The Oasis of Chenini-Gabes is crossed by a delightful lane that winds between dense palms and high frond fences through to Chenini. Beyond the Zawia of Sidi Abdesselem, which the local Boy Scouts recently vacated and the Zawia el-Ferjania adjoins, a Roman dam still controls the waters of the broad oued. This once-peaceful corner of antique cultivation is now hard-pressed by souvenir booths and, since 1974, exploited by the zoo. The walk up through the orchards to the two higher dams (one Roman, one 1895) is not far – and so charming that one would not notice if it were. The drive on leads up to the cliffs with the classic bird's-eye view.

Chenini-Gabes, the Roman dam

113

Matmata, pit-home of the troglodytic Berbers

In a pit-home, milling corn

Matmata. Modern white homes and mosques rather mar the 'face-of-the-moon' effect that travellers once described. The scene none the less is still somehow unreal: a broad saucer of raw earth, spiked with palms and pock-marked with the craters of some 700 pits. The Matmata Berbers, historians say, built their pit-homes to escape the notice of their enemies. An enemy that failed to see these gaping basins, however, would have been no match for the warlike Berbers who, once spotted, would have been sitting targets in their virtual tombs. A practical explanation seems more plausible: that the mountains' soft cohesive soil was harder to build with than dig into, and that the Berbers here, like the Romans at Bulla Regia, found subterranean homes the best defence against the heat of summer.

The inhabitants were no mere trogs but surprisingly sophisticated pit-dwellers whose underground constructions were a decided advance on the walled-up caves of their neighbours overhead. The pits are circular and about 30 feet in both depth and diameter. An entrance tunnel starts some distance away (to allow a gentle slope) and usually has chambers off for the animals. In the walls of the *haush* (the courtyard) are the remarkably snug rooms, twenty feet long, well insulated but inclined to collapse if rain loosens the soil. Spikes in the walls, or a knotted rope, help one up to the next 'floor'. Upper-storey rooms have shafts through the roofs as chutes for new deliveries of cereals and olives. Alcoves in the walls take beds and, if more shelves are needed, they can simply be hacked in the wall. Housewives, gorgeous in red or blue futas and black bakhnugs, still grind corn or couscous in millstones used since time immemorial. But with rising living standards in recent years, their families' living quarters have also literally risen: to the new street-level settlement where, to a man, the inhabitants have surfaced from their subterranean world.

Kebili, made a governorate in 1981, has in consequence mushroomed from a (Tuesday) market-village to a desert county-town. On the fork through town, beyond the Governorate, the old Dar ('House of') Bourguiba became in 1986 the Museum of National Liberation. From 3 September to 2 October 1934 it had been the penal stop-over in which the (then future and now ousted) president was held en route for the French penitentiary at Borj Leboeuf.

Douz was a desultory settlement that used to wake only weekly for the picturesque Thursday market. But latterly it has responded to tourism; first with hotels then, since 1976, with the Festival du Sahara, three mid-winter days of camel parades, races and fights, lectures, playlets, dances and displays of Beduin crafts.

The Romans, ubiquitous, installed themselves on these islands of greenery between the Chott el-Fejaj and the larger Chott el-Jerid, the 'Shore of Palms'. The banks of the chotts were once supposedly

Camelteers, timeless

covered in jungle, its denizens rhinoceri and hippopotami. The Nefzawa tribes have traditionally owned the oases, and the frequent Negroes survive from the days of the Saharan slave-trade, abolished only in 1862. They were much in demand as labourers because of their natural immunity to malaria, which the palm-groves' stagnant water made endemic.

For what counts here is less people than palms: 800,000 trees providing dates to eat, *laghmi* (palm-wine) to drink, stones to crush into ersatz coffee or fodder, fronds to make thatch and furniture, trunks to build roofs and foot-bridges, and fibre to weave into rope. If the oasis-dwellers live to a large extent from the palm, they also give it much of their working lives: boring wells to water it, pruning it in its 50-year rise to maturity and even pollinating it.

Chott el-Jerid. From Kebili

across the chott, tarmac was in 1984 completed to Degache and Tozeur. It removes the temptation (until lately Hobson's Choice) of driving delight-fully across a flat expanse of salt with no need to brake or even really steer. But still the route leads through an eerie landscape often as much mirage as reality. In places where winds (and the roadbuilders) have not heaped sand close, pools appear – the depths blue and green, the white shallows edged with pink.

The annual Sahara Festival, Douz (left)

Douz, the cemetery of the
Mrazig beduin (above)
The Chott el-Jerid (centre)
Oasis of date-palms near Douz (below)

Gafsa, the palms of the Roman pools and minaret of the Great Mosque

Gafsa and the Jerid. In a
land where living is hard and very
hot, and where the inhabitants seem
to take no great pride in their appearance, it is perhaps surprising
to find beautiful building. Yet the
simple towns of the Jerid have developed styles often more attractive
than British red-brick or Continental
stucco. The people of Tozeur and
Nefta have taken the common sand-
brick and worked it in bold geometric patterns that make the front
of the poorest home an object
of interest.

Gafsa, county-town of the same-
named governorate, is also the
region's natural capital. The species
of homo sapiens known as Capsian
Man takes its name from Roman
Capsa. Initially a Berber stronghold,
the town was first burned by Marius
in his successful campaign of 106 BC
against Jugurtha, then under Trajan
made a prosperous colonia (as is
evidenced by the Roman pools and
a mosaic found in 1969). The Byzantines renamed it Justiniana and
evangelized so effectively that, despite the Muslims' capture of its
80,000 inhabitants in 668, the

Gafsa from the Great Mosque minaret

118

population continued to speak Latin for another 500 years. In 1434 the Hafsites built the kasba, which withstood Dragut's siege of 1551 but succumbed in 1556. In 1943 the town changed hands three times, but less damage was done by the fighting than by an explosion in the French arsenal which laid low much of the kasba.

Of Gafsa's two Roman pools, the smaller has just-legible Latin inscriptions above the aperture from which the mineral water used to spout. The larger is more photogenic with the three arches of the Bey's Palace as one of the irregular sides, and the palm-trees and postcard minaret opposite. (The boys are up the trees and diving in before one can pull out a coin.) Past the antique capitals of the palace portico, the short walk up unlovely alleys is made worth while by the Great Mosque (a vast courtyard restored in 1969; columns straight, spiral or fluted, some Roman, some slotted for bolts, and an octagonal drum on the square minaret with a panorama of the town and its oasis).

Gafsa has an ancient reputation for weaving, which can be seen in progress at the ONA workshop. In a hive of activity (but parrot-house of chatter) some 200 local girls produce surprisingly fine designs, from traditional nursery patterns that defy Muslim tradition by depicting human figures, to roundelay pastiches of William Morris minstrels.

The Selja Gorges are the crack in the cliff face just visible from the Tozeur road after Metlaoui. The narrow-gauge railway that runs through them is a small engineering miracle, and the best means of admiring the equally wondrous scenery. Cut 500 feet sheer in the Selja Plateau, the gorges narrow into yard-wide defiles and widen into broad green corries that are awe-inspiring. The Romans, inevitably, left their mark in the shape of now-crumbling dams; snakes and scorpions account for the present lack of habitation.

The Selja Gorges

Tamerza is reached by a track from El-Hamma through desert mountain scenery. Fording the Oued Tamerza – the locals' Oued el-Khanga (the Defile) – it crosses Nouvelle Tamerza to follow the river-bed alongside the derelict but picturesque old town. From the second track that zigzags out of the oued, the view back might be the Yemen with its palms and crumbling qubbas.

Chebika is a 'model' mountain oasis: olives, palms, henna plants and pomegranates green against the pink coxcombed cliffs. From the 'roadhead' above the oasis, cliff-canals of clear water lead up through clefts and crevasses to the Selja-like corrie whence it falls.

Mides bestrides the next valley after Tamerza, and is served by the track left of the old Customs fort. The once-Roman Mades is made unforgettable by the gorges of the Oued el-Oudei. A path through the ghost-town of Old Mides climbs to a point overlooking the spot where three awesome canyons converge.

Chebika

121

Tozeur, approached from Gafsa, begins as a band of green along the chott. This gives way to the buff of the low-lying town which only three minarets distinguish. But Tozeur's far more distinctive feature is soon very striking and clear: arcades and façades on homesteads and mosques in baked-symmetrical, dusty-ochre brick.

If Jerba was somewhat 'un-Tunisian' in the south-east, here in the deep south-west Tozeur is almost equally so. The town may have had the expected Roman origins (as the outpost of Tusuros on the Gabes-Biskra road) but its dark-skinned Berbers were unusually fervid Christians and withstood the Muslim invaders for almost a century. Then they, like the Jerbans, turned to a minority sect of Islam, ascetic and mystic Sufism.

Tozeur rugs reproduce in wool the brick-designs of the buildings. In one arched and close-bricked alley of the 14th-century medina, the 'Archaeological and Traditional Museum' occupies since 1979 the Zawia of Sidi Ben Issa. The courtyard of worn capitals contains a headless torso (a marble Juba II – Cleopatra's son-in-law), giant pitchers for dates and/or oil, and Roman columns and capitals labelled 'Roman columns and capitals'. Beneath the qubba are circumcision costumes and Arabic books, in a side-room muskets and powder-horns, Beduin silver, furniture and clothes. Black African statuettes are explained by the presence here of 19th-century slaves. The 'bride's room' is appropriately pretty with silk screens and curtains, cosmetic trinkets and dress.

The oasis of Tozeur is watered by approximately 200 springs flowing at 165 gallons per second into mainstreams from which 2590 acres are strictly rationed . . . all this in accordance with a system laid down in the 1270s by Ibn Chabbat (and only in 1911-12 set down in writing by the French *contrôleur civil*).

The Dar Chraiet Museum, Tozeur: patio and faience (facing page)

Mosque of Sidi Abid, Tozeur

Tozeur rugs and runners

Tozeur, the oasis

Nefta appears at first to be just
another stretch of green beside the
chott. But this is an artificial oasis of
300,000 palms made possible by the
boring of 2100-foot wells in the 1960s.
The original oasis of Roman Nepte,
with its 152 springs, is dominated
by a hilltop called the Corbeille. The
classic sweep of the buff terraced
slopes, topped by domed marabouts and descending to dense
palm-groves, is perhaps the love-
liest of Tunisia's oasis landscapes.

Crafts and activities

Tunisian carpets, a traditional craft, are chiefly of the type that the Turks brought from Persia. The Beduin family's herds of sheep and goats provided the raw material, and the womenfolk the work. This began in spring when the sheep were sheared; the rising heat of summer then dried the washed, spun wool, along with the herbs, roots and fruit that provided the dyes. Natural dye-stuff went out with the Second World War, and home wool supplies could not long keep pace with the thriving industry that weaving soon became. Beside the ubiquitous workshops per se, every large bazaar from Bizerta to Tozeur has girls on low benches at tall looms working (and chattering) for eight hours per day. They use knotted point, with 10,000-490,000 points to the square metre. Only on Jerba are carpets and rugs made, mostly by men, in short nap. Most popular, the *zerbia* predominates. Its discreet geometry and subdued natural hues were evolved in Kairouan in the 1830s. The *mergum*, too, originated there, when the Zarrouk family thought of copying on carpets the patterns embroidered on the Berber women's bodices. The rugs and covers of Gafsa and Gabes are unmistakable in their nursery colours and Paul Klee motifs. All are called loosely *klim* or *hanbal*, though the latter is strictly a blanket, a Berber wedding-present in natural-coloured wool, and the *klim* traditionally anything red.

Wool-dyers, Le Kef (above) and carpet-weaving, Gabes

'Sidi Bou Said' bird-cages

Copper and brassware are incised skil-
fully, even to order, in every suq and
bazaar. The wrought-iron workers, in
Nabeul especially, forge items that look
too barbecue, but Tunisian bird-cages are
catching on even in European capitals at
multiplied prices. These blue-and-white
delights of ornate wire and wood are
now made as often in Raf-Raf as in
their namesake Sidi Bou Said.

Earthenware provides the widest and
cheapest range of Tunisian specialities:
glazed plates inscribed in Arabic (or
with camels and palms); beakers, lamp-
shades and plain ingenious ash-trays;
monstrous urns and shapely pitchers
four feet tall; dinky musicians ruddy-
buff in terracotta; elegant dinner-ser-
vices, gross glossy ducks and cocks
as tureens or table centre-pieces.
Nabeul makes most but from Guellala
come some pretty curiosities. The
potters work in three grades of clay:
cheap reddish buff, better creamy white
and fine grey kaolin. On the glazed
ware, patterns are traditionally flowery
or birdy and the colours green, yellow
and manganese-brown, though
Nabeul's potters are now turning
their hand to anything that sells.

Beduin bangles and fine filigree gold or
silver (*métal argenté*) are good value. On
every ancient site one is offered Roman
and Byzantine coins, openly by the
locals and surreptitiously by the official
gardien. Should any be authentic, the
price will be high. Most will be cheap
because labour is too – present-day
labour, in the back-room 'mints' of Tunis. And *caveat emptor*, 'buyer beware'
of the 'Roman oil-lamps' everywhere:
had the Ancients really left behind all
the lamps one sees for sale, they must
have used them much as we do
matches.

Index